Enculturation 485:
Immigrants Face the Realities
of Living in the USA

Enculturation 485:
Immigrants Face the Realities
of Living in the USA

Joan-Yvette Campbell

"Angels shine from without because their spirits are lit from within by the light of God"
~ Eileen Elias Freeman

dedicated to
CAROLE V. CAMPBELL –
"an angel in disguise"

Table of Contents

Preface

Leaving one's country to reside in another is usually a difficult decision to make. Starting a new life in another country is frightening and challenging for many. However, immigrants who migrate to the United States will make all effort to understand and adapt to the new culture even if they may not speak English. A language barrier does not stop immigrants from wanting to achieve the American dream.

The contributors to *Enculturation 485* are immigrants who represent different countries and cultures. Their input shows they may have gone through one or a number of adjustment phases where they are trying to overcome any challenges that may prevent them from adapting to live in the United States. Through their adjustment efforts, these immigrants uncover how their expectations prior to residing in the United States are different from their experiences and/or observations. Their reactions show that adjusting to a new way of life is not as easy as initially expected.

Through a number of topics in *Enculturation 485*, immigrant contributors provide their candid perceptions of the American ways of life. Each topic details an immigrant's cultural awakening on an issue and how such insight compares to behaviors in their native countries. Their reactions often initially indicate unfamiliarity with certain common practices of Americans. Some of the common practices include racial profiling, coping with mental illness, disciplining children, wage theft, and other important topics. Topics also uncover that immigrants from various ethnic backgrounds are more likely to face a number of challenges. The contents of *Enculturation 485* contain website addresses and other references that will provide immigrants and other readers with resources they may use to obtain further information on a particular subject.

Introduction

Many people around the world are captivated by what they are told about the United States. They are influenced by visiting friends and family who paint a rosy picture of life in the United States. These visitors may give an enticing impression that attracts especially those who have been experiencing economic hardships or other problems that will cause a desire to migrate. People, eager to leave their countries, may also be lured by cable televised programs and advertisements from the United States that show images of attractive people, beautiful clothes, expensive cars, inexpensive food , jewelry, and other products. They also see beautiful houses, skyscrapers, and places that seem unreal. They are amazed that residents of the United States seem to have it all. People are fascinated with a country regarded as a "land of milk and honey" where they feel life will be better since there are too many opportunities for all to succeed. However, the belief that it will be easy to adapt to living in the United States indicates the false impressions many conceive about residing in the country. As a result, people experience culture shock which often leads to disappointments with misconceived notions about life in the United States.

Noted reasons for coming to the United States include the following:

- Reuniting family members by filing papers for legal residency in the United States. This method allows the family to become the original structure of an American born generation in the future.

- Seeking economic opportunities appeal to many from developing countries where high unemployment, inflation, budget deficits are some issues that create financial hardships which ultimately affect the quality of life.

- Desiring educational opportunity influences persons' decisions since it is challenging to gain acceptance to limited universities in their native countries. Instead, they see that they will have a better chance of completing their post-secondary studies in the United States where there are so many higher education institutions which are regarded as more prestigious.

- Looking for political asylum is considered to gain admittance into the United States for those who fear imprisonment or death as a result of opposing political beliefs in their native countries. Petitioners are aware that living in the United States will allow them the freedoms that they have been denied in their native countries.

- Escaping from being the next casualty in their war torn countries encourages many to want to reside in the United States so that they may live under safer conditions.

- Possessing technical skills that are needed by a branch office doing business in the United States will cause the employer to file for an employee to be transferred to the United States office.

People from different nations will endure whatever travel difficulty or financial burden they may undergo to get to the United States. Therefore, they generally make up their minds to forego any obstacles prior to and during the journey. In some instances, people will go through the costly United States visas application process by getting up at the dawn of day and waiting in lengthy lines only for their Visitor's visa applications to be denied by an immigration officer. These applicants lose financially from paying expensive, non-refundable visa application fees in addition to facing disappointment from not obtaining a visa. Since going through the legitimate process of obtaining a visa may not be successful for some applicants, they may seek illegal options by land or sea that could lead to entry or detainment or deportation or death. Whatever the method of entry into the United States, if and when the immigrant arrives successfully into the country, he or she is more than likely to be confronted with culture shock and experience difficulties in adapting to a new way of life in a strange land very different from their own. According to Diakanwa (2011), immigrants have a difficult task integrating into the United States, and they will need to go through a period of adjustment. In the process of adjusting, Diakanwa, (2011) mentions that immigrants will have to go through Trivonorvith's adjustment stages as noted below:

- During the honeymoon stage, the newly arrived immigrants are usually thankful and happy to accomplish a dream to arrive in the United States. Such excitement makes them curious to want to learn more about their future life experiences in the United States.

- Next, the immigrant experiences the hostility stage where they begin to notice the realities of living in the United States. During this stage they encounter feelings such as frustration, nervousness, negative criticism, fear and depression. Non-native English speakers are even more affected than an English speaking immigrant since they may become frustrated with the difficulties of learning a new language. These immigrants along with others will begin to compare their own customs with their experiences living in the United States. They begin to notice the differences between their culture and the American ways of life. However, they will still make all effort to get adjusted to a fast-paced lifestyle if they reside in the city despite any illness that may impede some of their progress. The difficulties in adapting often cause an immigrant to develop a negative impression of the United States and a fear that he or she will not be able to succeed. Such obstacles may cause a desire to give up and simply return to the native country.

- The integration stage highlights the desire of some immigrants to persevere against all odds and make all efforts to adapt to the new environment. They become involved by learning about the culture, political, legal and other important systems within the United States.

- At the final stage, the home stage, the immigrant begins to feel at home and determines that he or she will continue to reside in the United States for the rest of his or her life.

Each chapter in ***Enculturation 485*** highlights various sub-topics that pertain to immigrants becoming familiar with the new culture. Chapter 1, *Adapting to a New Environment*, includes the reactions of immigrants that indicate their need to adjust to situations such as the cold weather, minority labelling, work conditions, credit system, and other aspects of life that are new to them.

Chapter 2, *Educational Issues*, contains references to sub-topics that readers should be aware of such as: educational opportunities taken for granted; school funding disparities; religious restrictions at public schools; distractions on college campuses; colleges that offer non-transferable academic credits; college athletic scandals, and other educational issues.

Immigrants featured in Chapter 3, *Cultural Differences*, bring awareness to cultural dissimilarities noticed by them that include humanizing pets, gentrification, and elderly disconnect.

Chapter 4, *Social Supportive Services*, provides immigrants' perceptions on homelessness, healthcare, housing, mental illness, welfare, and wage theft along with the resources to address these issues.

Chapter 5, *Impacted by Race and Gender*, presents immigrants' introduction to racial tensions and gender issues that continue to be prevalent in the United States.

Chapter 6, *Influenced by Politics*, depicts how immigrants look at politics in their native countries in comparison to politics in the United States. Subjects include the 1st and 2nd Amendments, religious inconsistencies, and the LGBT community.

Chapter 7, *Parental Challenges*, allows immigrants to share some of the problems they have experienced with their children who quickly adapt to the new culture. In addition, the chapter includes suggestions to encourage immigrants to take an active role in their child's education. Reprimanding children is another important topic that is covered in this chapter.

The compilation of immigrants' experiences or observations in *Enculturation 485* enables the sharing of information by accessing this single resource. It is hoped that the readings will be useful to immigrants while they continue to make all effort to adapt to living in the United States.

Chapter I

Adapting to a New Environment

Warming up to the Cold

Marcia is used to living in the Caribbean's warm climate. However, when she immigrated to the United States, she was looking forward to seeing the snow and wearing the fabulous winter fashions for the first time. But, during her first winter living in a New England state, she experienced a severe cold climate and a nor-east snow storm. Prior to immigrating to the United States, Marcia always saw beautiful, scenic pictures of a winter wonderland that looked so peaceful. However, no one told her of the layers of clothes she would have to wear; the frost bite she would experience while waiting outdoors for a bus that was never on time; that the snow could turn into ice, and this was a hazard for not only drivers but also pedestrians. She had no idea that the winter could include snow blasts with record temperatures well below zero. Marcia came to the conclusion that staying indoors and looking outside was the best way for her to enjoy the beauty of winter. She wondered if the residents living in her country really understood the difficulties immigrants such as her have to face in dealing with the harsh conditions of winter.

Adjusting to the cold weather is not an easy task especially for immigrants arriving from tropical countries (Letts, 2008). Immigrants who come from a tropical climate are accustomed to only rainy and sunny days. So, they usually have a difficult time adjusting, and they get sick easily when exposed to the cold weather. As a result, many immigrants, such as Marcia, do not enjoy winter time especially in areas where the weather is extremely cold. Furthermore, although immigrants may eventually get used to cold weather, they continue to remain uncomfortable with living in such cold temperature with chilly winds that can be quite unbearable.

While severe winter weather may be an expected challenge for people living in cold climates, new immigrants and recent arrivals often experience significant difficulty in adapting to conditions brought about by heavy snow, ice and wind storms, exposure to freezing temperatures, and power outages (University of Minnesota, n.d.). In December 2006, there were severe winter windstorms in central Washington State that carried winds gusting greater than 135 miles per hour. During the storm that lasted approximately one week, 1.5 million households lost power, and they relied instead on other methods to heat their homes and for cooking. Eight people were killed and more than 300 people were sickened by carbon monoxide poisoning due to unsafe uses of generators and grills indoors. Virginia Mason Medical Center in Seattle reported that out of the 70 cases of those treated for severe carbon monoxide poisoning, immigrants and/or people who spoke limited or no English accounted for the majority of patients. In fact, only five people spoke English as a first language. Cases of carbon monoxide poisoning during the central Washington windstorms occurred due to improper and unsafe use of alternative heating and cooking equipment. Since many of these immigrants who came from warm climates were accustomed to opening windows, they were not familiar with the danger of using grills and barbecue units in the home. More than 30 Somali immigrants who were treated had been using charcoal grills as sources of indoor heat.

Bidgood (2013) explains how unprepared some immigrants are when experiencing winter for the first time. For instance, at a winter workshop many did not know to remove their hats and coats when they entered the room of the workshop; they were inexperienced in navigating the icy sidewalk; however, one of the biggest winter issue is dealing with the temperature control inside an apartment.

According to Bell (2012) besides facing the novelty of fallen snow, immigrants are also bewildered by operating a furnace, steam radiator, and the high cost of heating oil bills. This lack of knowledge plus any language barrier can cause a conflict with a landlord. While housing laws such as in Maine require a thermostat in a rental to be kept at 68° F, many immigrants feel warm only with a temperature of 80° F and above. For more information on agencies that will assist immigrants in getting ready for the winter, see **http://www.acf.hhs.gov/programs/orr/programs**

Minority Classification

Many immigrants come from countries where their color or race or class or creed is dominant throughout the population. In their countries, they are used to seeing people who they can identify with in government leadership positions or working in other leadership professions that contribute to the development and progress of the country. However, living in the United States presents a new experience for those immigrants, such as Akiko, since she quickly became aware that she is considered a minority and has to identify herself within a minority category such as Black/African American or Latino or Asian or Native American. Akiko is of mixed race, so she checks the "Other" box instead.

Cohn (2014) reports that millions of Americans, who were counted in the 2000 census, changed their race or Latino origin categories when they filled out their 2010 census forms. Latinos, Americans of mixed race, American Indians and Pacific Islanders were identified among the groups who were likely to check different boxes from one census to the next. Research shows that these groups checked a different race or Latino-origin boxes than they did previously. Chaiklin, (n.d.) mentions that speculations on the changes are attributed to evolving self-identity or benefits associated with being identified with another group.

African Americans/Blacks were the nation's largest minority group. However, since the 2010 Census, it was discovered that Latinos have outpaced Blacks in population growth and have now become the single biggest minority group. While the Latino group continues to remain the largest minority group, the United States Census Bureau announced Asians were the nation's fastest-growing race or ethnic group in 2012. Their population rose by 530,000 or 2.9 percent, in the preceding year, to 18.9 million, according to Census Bureau annual population estimates.

The minority immigrant faces a number of challenges in addition to being relegated to a specific category. The term, ethnic minority, is often associated with prejudice and discrimination. According to

Chaikli (n.d.), ethnic minorities are often stigmatized as different from the norm. Religion, language, and, most significantly, skin color are quite likely to incite prejudice. To avoid being negatively singled out, many ethnic minorities try to quickly adapt to an American lifestyle with a change in their behavior, their outward appearance, etc. This demonstrates their great desire to fit in within the society.

Akiko surmises that hostility towards minority immigrants may come from those Americans most threatened. She knows that immigrants, like herself, want to succeed at any cost. Many will take work that may be regarded as unsuitable by an American. They will also accept work for low wages that may be unacceptable to a native born citizen. So, Akiko feels that while Americans complain that immigrants are taking their jobs, it is not often discussed that the immigrants are taking jobs that are rejected by Americans.

The minority immigrant's assimilation has depended on other factors such as skin color. However, Akiko believes that immigrants from countries such as India and Caribbean islands seem to have enjoyed economic success and social acceptance. For her, this could be perhaps because these immigrants have a homeland that they could easily return to and, they are not deterred by a history of dependency and discrimination. In addition, as native English speakers, language has not affected their ability to easily assimilate into society.

Restuccia (2014) mentions that by 2042 racial minority groups will make up the majority of the United States population. An extensive study on the shifting demographics indicates that within 1960 to 2060, the White Americans population will show a decrease from 85 percent to 43 percent. On the other hand, the Black and Latino population would have grown substantially over that same period making up 45 percent of the 2060 population. For more information on the changing demographics, see
http://www.pewresearch.org/fact-tank/2014/05/05/millions-of-americans-changed-their-racial-or-ethnic-identity-from-one-census-to-the-next/

Multi-Million Sports Industry

Stephen is a native of a country where athletics are an important part of the culture. Track and field and football are both implanted in the lives of the youth as far back as kindergarten. Stephen remembers that at an early age, he and his peers participated in competitive track and field events to win prizes at his school's annual sports day. Stephen also enjoyed playing football and had a sense of pride when selected for his school's team to play against members of other high school football teams. Another popular sport for him was playing cricket and cheering for the national team.

Stephen received an athletic scholarship to continue playing football and study at a university in the United States. He noticed the differences between athletics in his country and in the United States. For instance, football was called soccer in the United States. Soccer in the United States was not the number one sport as it has been in his country and so many countries throughout the world. He realized that the sport took a backseat to American football, basketball, and baseball. Learning about American football was not difficult for Stephen, and this knowledge allowed him to join in the fun by not only attending football games but also arriving early prior to a game for the tailgate parties. A tailgate party is a social event outside the stadium where fans gather before the football game to drink alcohol and grill food. On the other hand, while American soccer's popularity may not have captured great attention to be considered the primer sport of the United States like football, Stephen recognized an increasing interest especially during World Cup football. Furthermore, with the win of the United States women's soccer team in the 2015 World Cup tournament, the sport received a boost in its popularity especially among young girls.

Stephen also noticed that American football, basketball, and baseball professional athletes are highly paid. The 2014 Forbes listing notes that LeBron James's total earnings was $72.3 million which includes the biggest endorsements. Another basketball player's total listed earning was $61.5 million. The 2015 report on the highest paid football player is Ben Roethlisberger with a total of $48.9 million including endorsements. In contrast to the Major League baseball salaries with the minimum at $500,000, baseball players in the Minor League earn less than the federal poverty line. This could be around $11,500 for a single person or $23,500 for those with families (Berg, 2014).

Playing sports in Stephen's country or other developing countries does not generally offer great remuneration. To be highly paid, athletes would have to qualify to represent the country internationally. Those athletes whose success has given a boost to the country's brand not only receive substantial compensation but national honors, product endorsements, and their well-known status enables them to become financially comfortable for the rest of their lives.

Stephen recognizes that while sports in the United States represent a million dollar industry, issues exist that have resulted in litigation. College athletes are not paid although their participation generates wealth for the institutions. Also, the learning process of minority male athletes is undermined causing the focus to be placed on playing sports rather than dealing with a high rate of illiteracy. In addition, males are retiring from football with debilitating brain injuries that have resulted in death, yet parents still continue to encourage their children to play the sport. Women sports still seem to take a backseat to male sports despite laws to address the issue. For more information on important legal cases relating to sports including the National Football League's (NFL) players concussion litigation see **http://www.sportsbusinessdaily.com/Journal/Issues/2013/05/06/In-Depth/Lawsuits-intro.aspx**

Holiday Blues

Guy could not believe he had to work on Good Friday and even Easter Monday. Ever since he could remember, Easter was a holiday when the Christian majority population in his country began celebrations from the evening of Holy Thursday culminating Lent. They attended lengthy church services on Good Friday; returned to church on Easter Sunday morning; and continued the holiday celebrations on Easter Monday when it is customary for all businesses to be closed. So, Guy did not intend to work on the Monday after Easter Sunday since he was used to enjoying this day off. Guy did not expect that in the United States, Easter Sunday is the only day that seems to be recognized as a holiday. During Guy's first year of living in the United States, the experience of not celebrating Easter was annoying to him especially since he had made plans to leave town prior to learning that he would not have a long weekend off from work. In fact, it took Guy many years to get used to not celebrating Easter in the manner he grew to know.

Guy found that the popular holidays in the United States were different than what he was used to celebrating. For instance, Halloween and the practices were a new experience for him. He saw that the customs of Halloween activities include trick-or-treating with young ones walking from door to door collecting candies; attending costume parties; decorating; and carving pumpkins into jack-o'-lanterns. He wondered why people would go out of their way to dress up in costumes especially those with scary appearances.

Guy learned that festivities on the 4th of July clearly signify the country's celebration of the independence of the United States. He also became aware that the day commemorates the adoption of the Declaration of Independence on July 4, 1776, affirming independence from Great Britain. On this day, it is common to attend events such as firework shows, parades, barbecues, carnivals, picnics, and engage in other traditions. Guy enjoyed this type of celebration.

Thanksgiving is another popular holiday that was not familiar to Guy. He understood its significance with the pilgrims' arrival in Plymouth. According to the Smithsonian (n.d.), the colonists prayed and fasted for relief against a drought that was destroying crops. Rain fell a few days later. Not long after, Captain Miles Standish arrived with food, supplies, and news that a Dutch ship was on its way. As a result of these positive occurrences, colonists held a day of thanksgiving and prayer on June 30. Years later, this date was changed to the last Thursday in November. Guy knew that the symbolic practice on this day is to prepare a meal for family and friends, but the crowded supermarkets and lavish spending on food was an unusual experience for him the first year. But more unfamiliar to him the first year was Black Friday when massive sales are held at major stores beginning early in the morning to entice crowds of customers to shop for discounted items.

Christmas was always a special time for Guy. In his country, Christmas was celebrated not only one day, but the feeling of Christmas lasted through the month of December with so many festivities. Yet, the birth of Christ was always an important part of the celebration for him and his family. After giving and receiving gifts on Christmas Day, people looked forward to the next day, Boxing Day, a national holiday. He noticed, however, that Christmas in the United States is highly commercialized since consumers are bombarded with media advertisements to go shopping. Guy had to reluctantly return to work on the day after Christmas since it is back to business on December 26th in the United States.

Guy also recognized that while a day may be designated as a holiday in the United States, private companies can make their own decisions to open or close their businesses on that day. This practice is contrary to that of his native country where all companies will be closed. Guy also found out that there are less holidays in the United States than he was accustomed to celebrating in his native country. A listing of national holidays and their significance may be found on **https://blogs.anl.gov/newcomers/working-living-in-the-u-s/u-s-holidays-dates-significance/**

Utility Interruption Possibilities

Chishna remembers it was a common practice for all in his village to obtain water from a water drum. The small town had experienced regular water shortage due to the continued severe drought. Every year taps go dry as the demand from an increasing population rise. As a result, every morning, women with water containers queue up by the roadside to wait for the water truck. They sometimes had to remain all day for the truck that may or may not show up. Further, most of the water supplied is undrinkable so the water has to be boiled. Water restriction requests from the government and short term plans have caused the problem to persist for some time with no permanent solution. Chishna's family was so used to the lack of pipe water that it had just become a normal part of their everyday lives and this also extended to intermittent electricity. Now, life in the United States has been so different for Chishna. He certainly does not miss experiencing the discomfort of living without water and light practically every day. For him, it is a wonderful experience to know that day after day he can expect to have the comforts of electricity and water. He realizes that having water and electricity all the time is taken for granted by those residing in the United States since many do not stop to think what life would be like with the constant interruption of these necessities.

On the other hand, Jenell figured that since she now resides in the United States, she did not expect to experience power cuts or water lock off discomforts. After living in the United States for two years, she was now spoiled by uninterrupted utility services. However, she quickly learned that acts of God such as hurricanes, snow storms, etc. can cause the loss of electricity and even water for an extended period of time. In fact, according to Cohen (2005) approximately 2.5 million homes and businesses were in the dark as Hurricane Wilma pounded Florida during 2005. Jenell understands it is inevitable that power will be lost during such a severe storm. However, while she expects lengthy delays in the restoration of electricity in developing countries, she was surprised to know that such restoration delays also exist in the United States. She wonders why people would have to wait so long in a country where the state-of-the-art equipment should be readily available to repair power lines. During Hurricane Wilma, Jenell was more fortunate than others throughout the South Florida community who had to wait 2-3 weeks for the return of their electricity. Even with the assistance of out-of-state volunteer electrical repairmen, the task of restoring electricity lingered. For Jenell, the bottom line is that immigrants who are used to frequent power outage in their native countries cannot escape this problem even in the United States. Some who can afford to may avoid lengthy restoration of electricity by purchasing a gas-powered generator. However, Jenell believes that an immigrant's prior experiences will enable them to tolerate the temporary power and water loss with less difficulty in comparison to those who have grown up with the comforts of always having these necessities. For instance, her American friends were constantly complaining that the loss of electricity was especially unbearable without a functioning air conditioner. Jenell did not grow up with the comforts of living or going to school in air conditioned rooms, so doing without was not a big loss to her.

Power outages identify people's dependence on electricity. Nevertheless, to make life comfortable during those periods, it is important to stock up on essential supplies such as flashlights rather than candles that pose the risk of causing accidental fires. A battery-powered radio is necessary to stay alert on important news. More preparation information may be found on **http://www.accuweather.com/en/weather-news/how-to-survive-an-ice-storm-po/20680035**

Creditworthiness

Reynaldo was accustomed to using cash to make his purchases. He developed this habit while living in his native country where residents typically used cash to pay for items. If the residents did not have money to make costly purchases, then they would borrow money from family or friends or do without the product until they managed to save or secure the funds. Also, some major stores offered customers the opportunity to make a down payment and sign a contract to pay monthly. As a result of the high interest rates charged for this type of purchase, it was common for many people to save instead towards making such costly purchases rather than having a significant debt. Reynaldo shared that another popular method used to save towards purchasing products in his country has been for residents to come together and form a savings club. A designated member of the group serves as the banker who collects and disburses monies according to a weekly cash withdrawal schedule.

Reynaldo notices that credit is a popular method of payment in the United States. He understands that even if a consumer possess the cash to pay for a product, it is still necessary to establish his or her credit so that he or she will have a credit record that will determine their creditworthiness in the business and financial world. It was not easy for Reynaldo to obtain a credit card at first since his initial application for a bank credit card was rejected. Instead, he started his credit by obtaining a secured bank credit card. A secured credit card requires customers to deposit monies in an account that is equal to the credit limit. Once the customer demonstrates their creditworthiness, then the secured card may be converted to a standard credit card, and the customer will gain access to the funds in the savings account. Johnson (2014) informs that although the United States is expected to be the land of opportunity, establishing credit for immigrants is a big obstacle. Until they establish their credit, it is difficulty to easily obtain a credit card, rent an apartment, buy a car, or purchase a house. In Reynaldo's case, his outstanding repayment record allowed him to convert to owning a standard credit card.

While having the ability to use credit for purchases is a good method for Reynaldo to obtain items immediately and pay at his convenience, he is aware that irresponsible use of credit cards can lead to uncontrolled debt. Steinmetz (2014) reports that a survey by Bankrate.com found that nearly 30 percent of Americans have more credit card debt than they have in savings. For instance, people who lost jobs and homes during the recession had no choice but to use their credit cards for their daily living expenses. Furthermore, college students tend to increasingly use credit cards to finance not only living expenses but also their education. In 2009, Sallie Mae reported that 92 percent of undergraduates used their credit cards to pay for tuition and textbooks (Singh Miller, 2011).

Reynaldo also learned that a credit card is not the only form of payment that consumers need to worry about. It is also necessary that on time payments must be made for the rent, utilities, phone, and to any other debtors since creditors send customers' payment information to credit bureaus to add to a customer's credit history. This credit history includes a score that will identify the consumer's creditworthiness. Therefore, it is important to put bills in one place to avoid forgetting about them. Reynaldo also became aware that if unforeseen circumstances occur and a bill cannot be paid, it is better to contact the creditor to discuss options so as to avoid the creditor from implementing measures that will negatively affect the customer's credit for some time to come. Tips for building creditworthiness are located at **http://www.creditcards.com/credit-card-news/9-credit-building-tips-for-us-immigrants-1270.php**

Wear Out Welcome

Moise's father had filed immigration papers for him to obtain permanent residency in the United States. Moise was happy to know that his father was looking forward to him coming to the United States to finish high school and go to college. On the day of his departure from his native country, Moise's mother was very sad to see him go. She knew that she would miss her son, but it was in his best interest to have so many opportunities that are available in the United States. When Moise arrived in the United States, he was welcomed by his father, his father's wife and their two young children. Moise was pleased to see not only his father but to meet the other family members for the first time.

After a couple of weeks, Moise decided to start taking English as a Second Language (ESL) classes at a public technical school to improve his English and move on to college-related credit classes. However, as the months passed, his happiness in the house began to decline. Instead, there was tension especially when his stepmother was around. Unlike Moise's father, she did not believe that Moise should be going to school but felt instead that working would be a better option for him to support himself. There was constantly loud quarrels between his stepmother and himself, so Moise tried to spend as much time as possible away from the house. Furthermore, he became angry with his father who he felt was not defending him against his stepmother. Finally, the problems with his stepmother escalated to the extent that caused his father to have a physical altercation with Moise. His father asked him to leave, so Moise packed his bags and left. A friend's parents were sympathetic to his situation and allow him to stay with them. Since he was now on his own and needed to support himself, he got a job during the day and went to school during the evenings.

Moise's situation represents one of the many problems with immigrants moving to the United States. Often, people are sponsored by their family to migrate to the United States. Some leave a comfortable lifestyle in their homeland since they are lured by the promise that there are more opportunities in the United States to achieve a college education and a career. However, the honeymoon phase is over quickly for many. Sometimes when these immigrants arrive at the airports in the United States, they walk out of Immigration and Customs to a crowd of people but there is no one to greet them since their family is working or have other plans. These immigrants have to learn the system in terms of getting around town, enrolling in school, etc. since their families have no time to take them around town. Furthermore, children, such as Moise, may have to adjust to their father or mother's new family. As a result, children may have to adapt to a stepmother or a stepfather who may not treat them as equally as they treat their own child who was born in the United States. Often, immigrant young adults are turned out of the house and left to fend for themselves. Some decide to return to their native country to live with the other parent who does not waiver in showing them unconditional love. Some decide to stick it out and try to build a life on their own. Sometimes this situation leads to homelessness. The issue becomes even more difficult for those youth whose first language is not English because finding a job can be challenging.

Immigrants should be aware prior to coming to the United States that the friendly urging of parents, family, relatives, or friends to come to live with them may not be as welcoming after they spend a period of time with those persons. Immigrants should be mindful that many times, parents, family, relatives, or friends may not be available since they may have daily obligations. Therefore, the immigrant will be expected to learn the system on their own. Furthermore, immigrants should also know that if one parent remarries and starts a family in the United States, then the parent could be drawn into a conflict between the step-parent and the immigrant child. It is not unusual for the parent to take the side of the step-parent. Beware that the comfortable life expected may initially occur but the welcoming mat may quickly fold up. Resources in coping with family difficulties may be found at **http://homeless.samhsa.gov/resource/localresources.aspx#Florid a**

Nepotism and Legacy

Nepotism is prevalent in Manny's country, and he always disliked the practice. In his homeland, nepotism was embedded in the culture of the nation. A couple of his classmates, who were never high achievers, were assured of obtaining top level employment in their families' businesses or through family connections. There were never any doubts that these privileged individuals would secure the best jobs. Manny explained that nepotism was also blatantly evident even with government officials. The presiding head of the country has usually appointed top ministerial and government board positions to friends who were supportive during the elections. Often time, inexperience and on-the-job errors of these appointees have overshadowed any efforts to perform effectively, and this has led to great criticism from the media and the population. Furthermore, Manny expressed his discontent and frustration that those qualified job seekers who have been searching assiduously for long periods without success are lead, like himself, to seek opportunities outside the country. Therefore, although Manny loves his country and did not want to migrate, he had to do so in order to achieve opportunities that were not available to him in his native land. He felt that he would not have to deal with such unfair practices in the United States since he was of the impression that a person's degree, experience, and other abilities to do the job would be the main factor of employment.

After living and working at a government office in the United States, Manny realized that he had not left nepotism behind in his native country. In fact, he learned that this action was prevalent not only in local and state government offices but also the Federal government offices. Immigrants should be aware that nepotism is practiced greatly in some working environment in the United States more so than others. They will not be able to avoid the reality that whatever the country, human nature will lead people holding prominent positions to show favoritism towards friends and family by influencing the hiring process. This type of action promotes the saying, "it is not who you know, but who knows you". For instances, according to Swarts (2015), the head of the Justice Department's

International Criminal Police Organization (INTERPOL) told his staff to give extra attention in the processing of his son's job application so as to "earmark a spot" for him in the office. To make matters worse, Swarts (2015) reports that the Executive Director also made requests for employment of three of his son's friends although he had personally not met two of them. Furthermore, this federal department has been investigated throughout the years on the same issue of selected favoritism for job applicants. In another case, a City of Miami Parks and Recreation employee reported nepotism within her department. The employee claimed that the Assistant City Manager's half-brother and sister-in-law who recently arrived from Cuba not only obtained jobs within the department but made more money than the claimant and other employees who had decades of employment with the City of Miami (Green and Rabin, 2013). Even the Assistant City Manager was said to have received his job as a result of nepotism since he was reported to be a god-son of the mayor of Miami. It took the bravery of this Miami informant for an investigation to uncover the flagrant abuse that existed by creating jobs for inexperienced persons and even adding persons' names to payroll for them to only qualify to obtain health insurance.

Legacy is another preferential treatment practice that Manny found to be common in the United States. He was not familiar with the term "legacy" until residing in the United States. He found out that legacy is the process of accepting an applicant for entry into a prominent school based on their family connections to the institution. He realized that the legacy policy has been used as early as the kindergarten years of a child for selective entry into a prestigious preparatory school. Lewin (2011) mentions that family connection is considered even for admissions to prestigious colleges. A study of admissions at 30 highly selective colleges identified legacy applications. Therefore, at a time when an admission to a prestigious college is competitive, family connections are generally considered rather than the applicant's merit (Lewin, 2011).

More information on nepotism policies are found at **http://employeeissues.com/nepotism.htm**. Legacy questions may be answered by clicking on **http://collegeapps.about.com/od/theartofgettingaccepted/f/legacy -admissions.htm**

On the Road

Marva was used to driving her car in a country where following road rules is not the norm. Drivers seem to always be in a hurry as they speed and overtake lines of traffic even on single lane roads. Motorcyclists and bicyclists appear to have no fear as they merge from side streets without stopping. Pedestrians nonchalantly walk on the roads with no care for their safety. Further, there is chaos with the public transportation system. Buses exceed the maximum passenger capacity; passengers have to listen to blaring music whether or not the music is suitable for the public to hear; drivers speed, well over the limit, to compete to pick up passengers; and people ride in unlicensed taxis. The unlawful atmosphere depicts the overall indiscipline on the streets. Marva often wonders how some drivers managed to get a license since they follow no road codes and show no respect for the safety of themselves or others. From time to time, she saw that the police were present to set road traps. But, bribing the police with money would make any traffic ticket easily go away. Also, Marva found it more disturbing that the streets were so poorly maintained. The pot holes or craters, as they are popularly called, have caused extensive damages to many vehicles. Since sidewalks are not common, pedestrian often fall and sustain injuries when walking on the unpaved street surfaces. Yet, Marva is grateful that in her country she had the opportunity to not only learn to drive but to own a car since many people cannot afford to purchase an expensive vehicle.

While living in the United States, Marva quickly realized that the public transportation system was unsatisfactory because she not only had a lengthy wait, but after boarding, the bus took a long time to get to her destinations. Marva, however, was surprised with the way commuters lined up to board the bus which was contrary to the behavior of passengers in her country. Nevertheless, she did not intend to continue using the public transportation system for too long. Soon, she paid for drivers' education classes and began learning to drive in the United States. Learning to drive in the United States was harder for her than she expected since she would have to give up her familiarity with driving on the right side of the road and learn instead to drive on the left side of the road. Further, she had to get used to driving on a crowded highway during rush hour traffic.

Marva had to take the driving test twice before passing and obtaining her driver's license. However, the process of obtaining the license from the Department of Motor Vehicle (DMV) was not an unpleasant experience since she possessed all the documents that this government agency required. On the other hand, some immigrants have voiced their difficult experiences at the DMV. According to Lake, Snell, et. al (2006), immigrants report that navigating the DMV to obtain a driver's license is challenging especially for those with limited English proficiency.

Marva was impressed with how organized the roadway system was in her city and that most drivers seemed to follow the laws of the road. But, from news reports on road accidents, she realized that a number of people were driving with suspended licenses or no insurance or other traffic violations. She figured that some of these people were responsible for the hit-and-run accidents that occurred too often throughout the city.

Marva realized that purchasing a car in the United States was so much more affordable than in her country. She was warned, however, to take precaution prior to purchasing a used car by obtaining information on the value of the car in the Kelly Blue Book and also getting a mechanic to check the engine. She also learned that the value of cars in the United States depreciates immediately after they are sold and driven out of the parking lot of a dealership or from a private seller. In contrast, the prices of new vehicles maintained their value for a number of years in her country. She found and bought a car and enjoys driving it in spite of the fact that she has to now get used to pumping her own gas rather than having an attendant do it for her. Information on registered vehicles, transferring title ownership, obtaining drivers licenses, and all other vehicle related issues may be obtained at any local DMV.

Latchkey Kids

Joyce always enjoyed the daily bonding time that she made sure she had with her children. Both of her children would get home from school earlier than she did from work. But, once she got home she had the time to eat dinner with them and also assist with homework. She looked forward to weekends so that she could take her children to the movies, beach, or any fun activities. Joyce also lived in a community where neighbors know each other, so she was assured that they would look out for her children whenever they knew she was not at home.

When Joyce came to live in the United States, she often had to work long hours, so she came home sometimes when her children were asleep. She missed especially not always having an opportunity to eat dinner with her children, discuss how they spent their day at school, and help with homework. While Joyce moved to the United States because it offered more opportunities for her children, she felt she was missing out on their growth because, as a single mom, she had to work to support them. A parent's priority is to work so that they may provide for their children. However, Joyce felt guilty that the time she spends working has affected the amount and quality of time spent with her children. According to the Bureau of Labor Statistics, low income families have experienced an increase in low-paying jobs, irregular work hours, and a need to work overtime or more than one job. As a result of long working hours and irregular work schedules, parents are spending more time away from their family (Devine, n.d.)

When Joyce's children left school, they came home to an empty house. She learned that such children are labeled as "latchkey" children. That means the children go home to a house or apartment where there is no parental supervision. According to the United States census, one third of all school age children are considered latchkey. The Census Bureau found that 15% were home alone before school, 76% after school, and 9% at night since their parents may have to work the night shifts. (Alston, 2010).

When Joyce lived in her country, she could rely on the neighbors to look out for her children while she was at work and vice versa. The community demonstrated an atmosphere that represented the saying "it takes a village to raise a child". In the United States, however, she could not rely on neighbors to watch her children because she had not established a close relationship with any of them. Apart from saying hello to her neighbors, it was not easy to engage in a lasting friendship. She was away at work most of the time and her neighbors were not seen after they closed their doors. Poon (2015) reports that one third of Americans admit that they never interact with people living next door to them. Furthermore, few Americans do not know their neighbors' names. Americans, especially those living in large cities, may often be too busy to make new friends (Priven, 2005). Some immigrants say that in the United States, it is common for people to smile, look friendly, offer to get together, and then walk away. Immigrants soon realize that this offer is generally superficial. Joyce surmised that she must adjust to living in the United States away from the close-knit environment that she left behind in her home land.

Joyce's co-worker, Belinda, works overtime too with her, and she is also employed at a second job. Belinda works another job because she intends to earn as much money as possible not only to pay her bills but to buy whatever her teenage son desires. She buys him the latest designer clothes, shoes, games, etc. Belinda believes that, as an immigrant child, her son will easily adapt to the American culture when he has the latest American products. Further, she mentions that purchasing products for her son helps eliminate her feelings of guilt for not spending more time with him. Yet, Belinda confessed to Joyce that her son was performing poorly in school and that she was called several times to speak to his principal and teacher about his performance and conduct in class which caused a suspension from school. According to Alston (2010) most teachers believe that the number one cause of school failure relates to children who are alone at home after school. The afternoon hours are considered the peak time when juveniles commit crimes. Also, unsupervised children are more than likely to spend their afternoons watching television, eating snacks, and fighting with siblings. But, without parental supervision, latchkey children were expected to engage in sexual intercourse, become depressed, drink alcohol, smoke cigarettes and marijuana (Alston, 2010). Joyce prefers not to work too many overtime hours so that she can spend quality time with her children. She believes that her children will have to earn whatever they ask for by maintaining good grades in school. Community agencies such as the Boys and Girls Club, YMCA, and other local after school programs are available for students. While spending time at these programs do not replace the time spent with parents, adult supervision is available to assist students with homework and to engage them in meaningful afternoon activities.

Balancing School With Work

Prior to arriving in the United States, Nadiedge expressed a desire to continue her education. Her first intention was to enroll in an ESL class to continue her English language studies. However, while attending class, her aunt began to pressure her into getting a job to help pay for her food and stay. The aunt's reaction was disappointing to Nadiedge since she had expected to initially focus on her education prior to seeking employment. She wanted to learn sufficient English and gain a high school diploma after completing GED classes. However, it seemed that she would not be able to accomplish her educational goals.

Nadiedge got a job at a fast food restaurant, but made all effort to continue going to ESL night classes. However, her work hours were so unpredictable that Nadiedge missed too many hours of class and had to drop out. Nadiedge is one of the many immigrants with good intentions to make use of the opportunities to obtain an education, but plans are thwarted by the need to gain employment.

Pedro wants to go to school and is doing all that is possible to continue but it is so difficult. He works up until 11:00 P.M. and takes the last bus home. He does not arrive home until after 12:00 A.M. When he finally gets to sleep, it is after 1:00 A.M. He awakes in time to take two buses to school so he can arrive on time for the 8:00 A.M. class. During class, he is tired but he makes all effort to concentrate because he wants to pass the class. Sometimes Pedro cannot wake up on time and misses classes because he is so tired. He does not want to abandon school, but if he is so exhausted that he cannot focus, then he believes he is wasting his time.

Michel was asked to leave his aunt's house due to his continuous disagreement with her. He had to live with a friend but after some months, he needed to find another residence. At one point, he was homeless. Finally, he sought housing at a homeless shelter. They provided him with food and shelter but gave him a 90 day time limit to get a job. In the meantime, Michel continued to attend an adult education center. But, he was aware that if he did not locate employment and housing within the 90 days, then he would have to drop out of school.

Manuel was enrolled part-time in an ESL class for over a year. It was so frustrating for him since it was taking him a long time to learn English. He was told that he needed to also practice learning English outside of the classroom. But, Manuel worked long hours and was too tired to put extra effort into learning English. Furthermore, he has a growing family and needed to work extra hours to take care of their needs.

Immigrants like Nadiedge, Pedro, Michel, and Manuel have good intentions to attend school so that they may make a better life for themselves and their families. However, their need to work quite often interferes with their plans to obtain an education. Unfortunately, many do not return to school and end up doing the same jobs for many years. Kantrowitz (2009) mentions that a study, by the Bill and Melinda Gates Foundation, found that the main reasons for dropping out of school have included conflicts with school and work and family commitments. Many who dropped out found that they had to work while attending school. They often realized that it was difficult to support themselves and their families and attend school at the same time. Nearly 71% of students poled indicated that work was one of the contributing factors for dropping out; 54% identified work as the major factor; 35% mentioned that balancing work and school was too stressful (Kantrowitz, 2009). Immigrants desiring to enroll in classes should check the offerings at the public school's adult education center or the local community college since these institutions provide a number of classes at different hours throughout the days, afternoons, and evenings that should fit a work schedule. Talking to an instructor or school counselor is also important because they may be able to suggest an option for students to continue attending classes. Another alternative for those experiencing difficulties in continuing their post-secondary education is to consider online classes because most community colleges and universities have undertaken this type of learning.

The Criminal Justice System

Mohammed came from a country of lawlessness where there was no recognizable criminal justice system. He was glad that he not only had an opportunity to migrate to the United States, but he was impressed with the country's organized criminal justice system.

Mohammed learned in class that, in the United States, an infraction is a minor crime. But, he could not believe that it was a minor offense to cross in the middle of a street which is known as jaywalking. Furthermore, he learned that such action is considered an infraction and may be punishable by costly fines. In addition, he became aware that other minor infractions include littering when people throw or dump trash in public places. Also, traffic violations are considered as infractions.

Misdemeanor is another crime category that Mohammed learned about. He was told that this type of crime is more serious than an infraction but less serious than a felony. Examples of misdemeanor include trespassing on private property. Mohammed did not know what shoplifting meant, but it was explained to him that this misdemeanor occurs when people steal items from stores. Persons who are charged with misdemeanor may be placed on probation or required to complete community service if they are first time offenders. On the other hand, consistent offenders may be sentenced to prison for one year or less.

Mohammed understood that a felony is the most serious crime. Examples of such crime would include aggravated assault, rape, murder, and other violent offenses. Mohammed also realized that there are various degrees of murder such as first degree where a crime is planned. Those accused of a felony generally receive lengthy sentences up to life in prison, or the accused may be sentenced to the death.

Mohammed is aware that the criminal justice system throughout the United States is complex. He noticed that there are some crimes where it would be natural for them to be considered as infractions yet the accused are sentenced to lengthy stays in prison. According to Sullum (2014), a 2013 report indicates that thousands of nonviolent offenders are serving prison sentences of life without parole. Furthermore, the American Civil Liberties Union (ACLU) provides information that there are a number of cases where people receive life sentences for marijuana offenses. One example is Weldon Angelos, who at the age of 24 years old, was sentenced to 55 years in federal prison for not only selling approximately 1 1/2 pounds of marijuana but for also possessing a firearm during the marijuana sale. On the other hand, a Texas teenager who was drunk when he drove into and killed four people was given a light sentence although he violated a number of laws. This teen, from a wealthy family, received 10 years of probation since the verdict supported his lawyer's claim that the teen did not know right from wrong due to his affluent upbringing.

In addition, Mohammed became interested in obtaining information about the Amendments to the Constitution as they relate to the criminal justice system. He noticed that the 6th Amendment protects the rights of the accused. Also, this amendment provides the right to an attorney for those who are unable to afford legal representation. The 4th Amendment offers protection so that law enforcement will present a warrant prior to searching a residence and seizing any contents from that dwelling. The Center for Immigration and Justice provides a number of websites for immigrants to obtain information on the criminal justice system and their rights. Such websites include:

- **http://www.vera.org/centers/center-immigration-and-justice;**

- **The Immigrant Defense Project http://immigrantdefenseproject.org/;**

- **Immigrants' Rights https://www.aclu.org/issues/immigrants-right.**

Invisible Immigrants

Sonia did not have to migrate to the United States. She had a professional career that paid not only a good salary but received perks for laundry, car maintenance, and other benefits. However, the rest of her family had already migrated. She missed not living in close proximity to them, and through their urging, she decided to leave. Sonia did not experience the difficulties as many in settling in the new country since her family had already established their lives in the United States. Soon after she obtained a job with possibilities of gaining a promotion.

After living in the United States for a period of time, Sonia believes that immigrants from her country and the other countries in the same region are invisible to local, state, and federal politicians. She surmises that the mention of the word "immigrant" is immediately associated with the Latino community probably since they represent the largest growing minority group in the United States. Even in instances when the DREAMers group is mentioned, many believe the activists are only Latino youth who were brought illegally to the United States by their parents. Such misrepresentation was demonstrated when a popular college held a press conference to publicize that the institution was offering DREAMers scholarships to continue attending school. While the college is located in a multi-ethnic city with Haitians representing the second largest immigrant group, all of the approximately 15 or so DREAMers on stage at the news event were Latinos.

Sonia thinks that there is a failure in the United Sates to recognize other immigrant groups besides the Latino community. She is aware that there are other groups of immigrants who have played a significant role in the financial growth of the nation. It is only recently that major hotel chains have been acknowledging the purchasing power of the Asian Indian community since these immigrants will pay whatever is necessary to have a wedding ceremony of a lifetime. Nair (2015) reports that major hotels are trying to woo Indian couples to select their hotel for a wedding that generally costs between $300,000 and $400,000. Yet, Sonia believes that if it was not for the extravagant spending of the Asian Indians, then this community would continue to remain invisible in the eyes of American corporations.

The number of English speaking immigrants such as those from the Caribbean is estimated since there is no specific category box for this group on the Census form. Sonia cannot understand how English speaking immigrants have no other choice but to check other categories on the Census form. So, the Census report that there are over one million Indians from Asia may quite likely be skewed since Indians from Caribbean countries and elsewhere may have also checked the box. Furthermore, the census on African Americans includes those Black immigrants from other countries. Sonia hopes in the future that there will be a Caribbean category on the Census form to provide a true population record.

Sonia also notices that while much attention is placed on obtaining the Latino vote especially during an election, she is disturbed that no great attempts have been made by presidential or other political candidates to attract the vote of hundreds of thousands of English speaking immigrant citizens. The politicians are oblivious that these immigrant groups listen to ethnic radio stations that not only play music but listeners are kept abreast of political news and are encouraged to register to vote. The hosts of the programs have great influence on the listeners. So, Sonia believes politicians are missing an opportunity to attract many new voters. Voting for politicians seems like a travesty to Sonia because she does not see any of them giving attention to issues or causes that relate to the non-Latino groups.

Sonia, however, is optimistic. She hopes that more citizens from her country and those from countries in the surrounding territories will get involved in politics as that is the only way their voices will be heard to gain representation. Further discussion on this matter may be found at **http://www.ibtimes.com/caribbean-americans-invisible-minority-seeking-identity-affirmation-795709**

Tax Returns

In Devon's native country, people pay taxes; however, he was self-employed and somehow avoided paying taxes for many years. But, like everyone else, he had to pay taxes on all purchases. Now that he lives in the United States he knows that he cannot avoid paying taxes.

Devon learned that he must pay Federal and State taxes. In addition, he found out that taxable income includes not only wages but also any monies that are made from self-employment and tips. Initially, he could not get used to so many deductions taken out of his gross pay. The deductions included Federal income tax, social security, Medicare, state taxes, and state insurance.

Devon also became aware that anyone working in the United States should file a tax return every year to report their income to the Internal Revenue Service (IRS). IRS is the revenue service of the United States federal government that is responsible for collecting the yearly income tax from residents and businesses. An employer is also expected to report their employees' income and deductions to the IRS. The employer must provide all employees with a W2 form that indicates the yearly income and deductions of the worker. If a worker's total Federal income tax deductions exceed the threshold, then he or she is expected to receive a refund. However, if the person's tax deductions fall below the threshold, then he or she will be expected to pay the shortfall to the IRS. After Devon received a refund of his taxes, he was no longer bothered by so many deductions from his salary since he had a tax refund to look forward to receiving each year.

The IRS performs random audits of tax returns to ensure that filers are complying with tax return laws. Some tax returns may be flagged for criminal investigation. Audit methods may also include selecting tax payers if their information does not match other records from their employer or if it appears that the taxpayer is trying to underpay taxes or if other red flags occur that is secret to the IRS. Evading taxes is considered a felony and could be punishable with imprisonment depending on the severity of the case. Over the years, many cases have been publicized of celebrities and wealthy persons who had to pay hundreds of thousands or even millions of dollars in back taxes or face going to prison.

Devon has seen that tax refund identity theft is a growing epidemic in the United States. In fact, the IRS ranked identity theft tax refund fraud as its number one scam. This crime occurs when someone uses a person's personal information such as their name, social security number or other identifying information without permission to commit fraud or another crime. Generally, the crime will involve filing a fraud tax return and claiming a refund early in the filing season so the refund will be received before the victim files his or her tax return. By the time the IRS is made aware of the crime, the thief has already cashed the refund check. Devon understands that tax payers have to be wary even of their tax preparers. In one case an accountant secretly prepared two different versions of tax returns. The accountant gave the accurate version to clients, and the fraudulent one, with a higher refund, was sent to the IRS. When the IRS paid out the refund, the accountant had the amount the clients were expecting deposited to their account while the rest of the money was pocketed. Taxpayer Assistance Centers are located in communities across the United States. To find a Taxpayer Assistance Center, go to **http://ww.irs.gov/localcontacts/index.html**

In Debt

Safi was not familiar with the credit card system until she came to the United States. Her only knowledge about using credit was that, as a child, when her grandmother sent her to the community grocery store, she received the items but never paid for them. Safi knew, however, that her grandmother paid at the end of each month when she received income from various sources. This exchange was called "trusting", and most of the people in the community did the same. The store owner knew all his customers and trusted that they would pay the accumulated bill. After moving to the United States, Safi realized that a more sophisticated type of credit system existed since the common method of making purchases was to use credit cards. She saw that consumers were used to purchasing what they wanted immediately and paying later whenever they received their credit card statements. Safi saw that this popular purchasing method has been made more enticing for consumers with the bombardment of product advertisements especially during holiday seasons.

Safi realized that it was important to establish credit in the United States. For this reason, after working for one year, she eventually applied and was approved for a credit card. This was the only credit card she wanted and turned down the other offers that were made to her when she went to stores or those she found in her mailbox. She decided from the beginning that she would use this credit card wisely by making only important purchases because she heard about the horror stories of people getting into difficulties by misusing their credit availability limits. Furthermore, she learned that banks made significant profits from interest charged to their customers who did not pay the full balances on their statements.

Certainly consumers misuse their credit cards when they are lured by advertisers to make purchases that many often cannot afford. However, consumers must be aware that credit card companies and banks benefit substantially when balances are not paid in full. The bad habit of making everyday purchases such as groceries, gasoline, etc. with credit cards causes consumers to pay for the items long after they are consumed. Also, when consumers pay only the minimum on credit card bills, they incur higher finance charges and the cost of whatever was purchased increases. In addition, cash advances from credit cards will cost a consumer dearly since the interest rates are much higher than the norm. An example of a predatory lender taking advantage of consumers occurred when a customer's interest rate started at 29.9% and increased after 6 months to 79.9%. In addition to credit cards, cash needy people are opting for payday loans or loans from other predatory lending agencies. One of many payday loan troubling stories includes a borrower whose payday loan quickly ballooned from $450 to $1,700 within a matter of weeks.

Many quickly realize that they are unable to pay back their credit card or loan debts, and this causes them to default. Not paying a credit card or loan and having a collection agency constantly calling can become not only an uncomfortable experience but also is overwhelming. This debt is about much more than money as it can lead to a number of psychological issues (Kuchar, 2014). Debt leads to depression and anxiety for many. News reports show the desperation of some debtors may even result in suicide.

Safi believes that credit card and loan counselling needs to begin while students are in school. They should learn how to use a credit card wisely and manage their debt. In this way, at an early age, they will become familiar with the advantages and disadvantages of using credit. They will be aware that it is not always wise to accept store credit card offers simply because they are lured by the discount they will receive on a one time purchase. Knowledge at an early age will enable students to develop the discipline that is required in handling the enticement of using credit cards and other types of credit offers. The website **http://www.consumerfinance.gov/** offers consumers information and services to assist with credit card and other loan issues.

Cash Workers

When Marco came to live in the United States, he was lucky to get a job since his cousin worked in construction. Marco was not used to such hard work, but he was grateful because he arrived in the United States during the period when construction had taken a down fall and, in fact, many people did not have a job. Marco thought that he was even more fortunate as he got paid in cash at the end of every week. He worked with the same employer for a few years before the construction project ended. Marco did not want to continue working in construction, and it took him a long time before he got a job as a custodian at a school. He preferred this job that was not as hectic as working in construction. However, he was not used to getting his pay every two weeks in the form of a check. Also, he was surprised the first time he received his pay when he noticed deductions for Federal Income Tax, social security, Medicare, and state taxes. At first, he was not happy that so much money was taken out. However, he realized that, in the long run, the deductions would be more beneficial to him since he could file his income tax and get a refund. Furthermore, he was pleased to know that paying social security would give him an opportunity to get a monthly income from the government when he retired. Knowing this made him wish that deductions had begun from the start when he worked at the construction company.

Gambone (n.d.) describes a cash worker as an individual who performs the services of an ordinary employee, but who is not actually hired formally by the employer. These workers are also known to work for employers who pay an employee "under the table". "Under the table" is a common idiom that describes the secretive nature of the work situation. In addition, these employers may incorrectly classify an employee as an independent contractor. Nevertheless, both the employer and worker may be blind to the fact that there are significant risks in hiring and being a cash worker.

The perceptions of employers who hire a cash worker is that they can avoid paying taxes and insurance expenses associated with payroll. Furthermore, employers are able to pay cash workers at a lower hourly wage than traditionally hired employees. Also, these employers are not obligated to provide any benefits to the cash workers (Gambone, n.d.). On the other hand, people may prefer cash work so that they will earn a larger income; their employment history cannot be traced so that they can continue to receive public assistance; monies will not be deducted from their salary for obligations such as child support; income tax cannot be deducted from their pay; and it is the only option for illegal immigrants who cannot gain legal employment.

Employers who are in the habit of hiring cash workers may not realize that they are compromising their business and the welfare of the worker. Foremost, paying employees under the table instead of using a formal system of accounting and payroll is considered illegal. Such a criminal offense is regarded as tax evasion or fraud which could lead to substantial fines or imprisonment since the action shows an intentional avoidance of paying employment taxes. Furthermore, workers who accept cash instead of a payroll check are hurting themselves because they have no legitimate proof of employment and income. Such undocumented work can prevent these workers from obtaining social services such as unemployment assistance or Social Security. They could also be charged with income tax evasion if the Internal Revenue Service discovers the under the table arrangements. Information on unreported employment is available at
http://www.edd.ca.gov/pdf_pub_ctr/de573ca.pdf

Lawsuit Frenzy

Lawsuits are prevalent in the United States. It seemed to Raynaldo that people sue for almost any issue. He saw that not only do people initiate law suits, but persons never know when they, themselves, may even be sued by others. There are many attorneys in his native country, but an average person would not be able to afford their services to file a law suit. But, in the United States, the plethora of attorneys and methods of filing law suits facilitate the public's need to get legal justice for their concerns. Raynaldo enjoyed watching court shows on televisions where people, representing themselves, are able to argue their small claims law suits without an attorney. He has seen landlords suing tenants and vice versa; neighbors suing neighbors; parents suing children and vice versa. The low fees to file a small claims' lawsuit have opened up the doors to the multitude of lawsuits throughout the country. Raynold believes that the simplistic reasons for filing some lawsuits have signaled how the practice has become an American way of life for so many. For instance, a $50,000 award was made to a litigant who sued a neighbor as a result of the barking of the defendant's dog. Further, a convicted bank robber sued the police force for $6.3 million for the shot he incurred while committing the crime. In addition, a recent graduate sued her alma mater for $72,000 when she was unable to find a job three months after graduating with a Bachelor's degree in Information Technology.

People may seek the services of an attorney to represent them in filing a complex law suit that they cannot handle by themselves. There are too many attorneys to choose from, so it is important that people take the time to find an attorney that they feel comfortable working with. Obtaining a referral from someone with a similar legal situation who was represented by an attorney would be helpful. Once an attorney is selected, it will be necessary to obtain a written retainer agreement from the attorney that provides details on the retainer fee, the work that will be performed, administrative and/or miscellaneous costs.

Filing a law suit with Small Claims Court may simply be done by downloading forms online. The lawsuit must be under $5,000. After completing the form with the problem, then a minimum court fee must be submitted with it. The person or company being sued may be notified by certified mail or have a server do it for a fee. If the case is not resolved through a mediator, then a judge will decide a verdict. The litigant and defendant may also hear from personnel at a television court show who expresses an interest in flying them to the broadcast studio in another state to tape the legal case. Both parties to the case must agree to take up the television court offer or, if not, the case will remain in the local court's jurisdiction.

Law suits may also be filed through government agencies such as the Equal Employment Opportunity Commission (EEOC). When workers believe that they are discriminated against at the workplace, then they may file a claim with EEOC by completing an application form online. The claim may be handled expeditiously by a mediator. However, the claimant may prefer the lengthy wait that it will take before the matter is turned over to an attorney. The Department of Justice may be contacted at **http://www.justice.gov/crt/how-file-complaint** to file a complaint or lawsuit.

Chapter 2

Educational Issues

Taking Education for Granted

Many immigrants, such as Ishmael, have expectations that going to school will be their key to opening doors to many opportunities. Various life circumstances affected or impeded some immigrants from obtaining an education in their native countries, so they will make all effort to go to school when they immigrate to the United States.

Ishmael stopped going to school at the age of 14 years when his mother died. He was expected to help support his two sisters and one brother while living with an aunt. He was a good students, so it was disappointing to him and his teacher that he could not complete his education. According to Brilliant Earth (n.d.), many, if not most child miners in Africa do not attend school. They are usually considered for employment in the diamond mining industry since they provide a cheap source of labor. Furthermore, in some areas of Africa, children make up more than a small part of the workforce. This life of hardship that requires they fend for themselves and their families does not provide any chances for schooling. Yet, some under privilege children are willing to experience great hardship to commute to school. For instance, in Sumatra, Indonesia, due to a collapsed bridge, children from Batu Busuk village have to tightrope walk 30 feet above a flowing river and then walk a further seven miles through the forest to get to their school on time in the town of Padang (Amusing Planet, 2013). In Columbia, some children living in the rainforest commute via steel cables that connect one side of the valley to the other. During clashes between the Palestinians and Israelis, students have to walk through war torn streets to get to school.

When Ishmael arrived in the United States, his difficulties in obtaining an education in his homeland made him wonder why students would take their education for granted by complaining about not wanting to go to school; arriving late to class; cutting classes; and dropping out. Education Secretary Arne Duncan (2009 – 2016) noted that although there has been a decrease in the dropout rate, it is still high and unacceptably in the African-American,

Latino, and Native-American communities (Homeroom, 2013). Some explanations for dropping out are as follows:

- They make poor decisions by getting involved with gangs, drugs/alcohol. Others get pregnant and some commit crimes. Many have a poor school attitude and are frequently bored by school. They are disconnected to their families, school, and life. They do not see the reasons they need to go to school. (Schargel, 2013)

- The students come from families of low socio-economic backgrounds where there may be a single parent caring for many other children. Some of these parents did not complete school so the cycle continues.

- Some children live in communities where drugs, gangs, and violence are valued instead of education.

- Low income communities receive less funding for schools rather than those in wealthier communities because funding is based on property value.

- The least experienced, least class-room trained teachers are often assigned to the most difficult schools.

Ishmael made a promise to himself that he would complete his education in the United States, and he has taken advantage of opportunities to do so. Further information on continuing education and other course offerings may be obtained from the local community college or adult education public schools throughout the neighborhoods.

School Funding Disparity

Janine came from a culture where a standardized test was compulsory at the middle school level in order to attend high school. A child's academic abilities determines placement in either a prestigious or unrecognized high school. She quickly learned; however, that the school system is different in the United States since she was placed immediately in a high school located near her home. When she came to the United States, she lived in a community that is considered the inner-city. The high school reflected the community of African Americans and Latinos. Janine was vaguely familiar with the 1960s ruling on Brown vs. Board of Education that was expected to end segregation of schools. She watched documentaries on how African American children such as Ruby Bridges risked their lives under police protection to desegregate Whites only institutions. Therefore, Janine wondered why, after so many years since the desegregation ruling, there seemed to be no changes in diversifying schools such as the one she attended.

Since Janine's last high school in her country was an all girls' catholic school, she was accustomed to this sheltered learning environment. Janine found that the classroom environment at the all girls' school was calm with no teacher/student confrontations that she could remember. So, hearing students cussing, shouting, and fighting in school was a new experience for her. As for equipment, Janine noticed the outdated equipment found inside classrooms for both teachers and students. Even more troubling to her was the overall poor maintenance conditions inside the school building. The computers used at her previous school in the developing country were far more updated. However, Janine kept hearing that all schools in the city were not in a dilapidated condition. When she had an opportunity to visit a public school located in an affluent residential area of the city, she noticed the vast differences. The population at this school was predominantly White. The facilities were well-maintained, and the common areas were immaculate. All the state-of-the-art equipment was available for the learning needs of the students. Furthermore, the swimming pool and modern athletic facilities made her wonder why all students in the United States were not equally offered a satisfactory environment to promote learning.

According to Donald (2013), a report on how to close the achievement gap includes that 10 million students in America's poorest communities are affected by an educational system that assigns them low-performing teachers, run-down facilities, low academic expectations and opportunities. Such so profound or systemic inequities were not identified in other developed nations. The report recommends for new teachers to be better trained, implementation of a school finance system that provides adequate funding for every child regardless of where they reside, and more support services for the poorest children and those with special needs. A Schott Foundation for Public Education reveals that the communities in New York where most of the city's Blacks and Latino students reside are negatively affected by policies and practices that give their schools the fewest resources and their students the least experienced and stable teachers. However, in contrast, the best-funded schools with the highest percentage of experienced teachers are often located in the most economically advantaged neighborhoods (Strauss, 2012). Further, the report indicates that students from low-income New York City families of all ethnic groups have little chance of being tested for gifted-and-talented program eligibility. Few Blacks and Latino students are selected for the city's top exam schools, such as Stuyvesant and the Bronx High School of Science. For more information on Brown vs. Board of Education see video
https://www.youtube.com/watch?v=TTGHLdr-iak

Undervaluing Foreign Degrees

Eduardo always wanted to become a doctor since he was a child. He achieved excellent grades in science subjects throughout high school and continued along that path when he entered university. After graduating, he was accepted into a medical school, then went on to a residency program at a hospital. Although he had a prestigious career, the political upheaval in his country caused him to decide to seek a better life in the United States since he already had family and friends living there. While living in the United States, he completed English as a Second Language (ESL) courses and worked hard to improve his English skills in anticipation of continuing in the medical field as a doctor. But, he found out that achieving such a goal involved a lengthy process with rigorous exams for those whose native language is not English. The successes he accomplished as a medical doctor in his native country did not matter.

Those immigrants, such as Eduardo, with professional backgrounds who are not native English speakers may come to the United States with great expectations of learning English so as to tackle the arduous process that is necessary to continue working in the profession that they were trained to do in their countries. However, learning English may be more challenging for some or issues may arise that interrupts the learning process and career goals. According to Rampel (2013), thousands of foreign-trained immigrant physicians who reside in the United States possess lifesaving skills but are unable to use the training due to the many challenges they experience toward becoming a licensed doctor. The process is tedious. Initially, foreign doctors must apply at a private nonprofit organization that verifies medical school transcripts and diplomas. Also, foreign doctors must prove English proficiency and pass three separate steps of the United States Medical Licensing Examination. In addition, they must obtain American recommendation letters by volunteering or working in a hospital, clinic, or research organization. Further, the immigrant must be permanent residents or receive a work visa. However, the most challenging requirement is for the immigrant to secure one of the coveted slots in America's medical residency system. They can only accomplish this goal by competing with native born American medical students for residency in spite of the fact that the immigrant doctor has already completed a rigorous residency program in their native countries. Some may succeed, but the challenges experienced force others to use their skills elsewhere at jobs such as nurse practitioners or physician assistants. Seeking other positions not only indicates a loss in status but also in the high income that is expected as a physician. They realize that they cannot continue to hang on to a dream that they will become doctors during their new life. It is a tough adjustment for most immigrants but in order to survive, they cannot be choosy of the job they will do to earn a living.

Similar to those skilled medical professionals, other professionals migrating to the United States have encountered difficulties. For instance, between 2009 and 2011, some 46,000 immigrants in Massachusetts, or 20% of the immigrant college-educated population, were either unemployed or worked in low-skilled and lower wage jobs that did not use their education and skills (Massachusetts Immigrant and Refugee Advocacy Coalition, n.d.). Furthermore, those who earned their degree in other countries may face even more difficulties. The report indicates that once these immigrants arrive in Massachusetts and elsewhere, they are confronted with many obstacles that prevent them from putting their degrees and skills to work. They may experience language barriers, unfamiliarity with United States work culture, and the complexity and expense of recertifying in their professions.

Yildiz, 2010 reports that the gap between skilled immigrants and natives is most commonly as a result of:

- Foreign academic credentials in the United States are undervalued or not fairly evaluated or too difficult to assess.

- Knowledge and use of foreign credential evaluation services is limited among employers and immigrant job seekers.

Information on immigrants and their foreign academic credentials may be found at **http://wenr.wes.org/2009/12/wenr-december-2009-feature/**. For a list of foreign credentials evaluation services, see **http://www.naces.org/**.

Fight Against Religion in Schools

Justine started going to church from a young age, so religion has always been an important part of her life. She was christened in the Anglican church which is known as Church of England in Commonwealth countries or Episcopal in the United States. Prayer in the middle school classroom or at assembly was an important daily routine that was expected every day prior to beginning classwork. Justine later attended a high school which was associated with her Anglican upbringing. Daily prayer was important, so all were expected to participate unless their religious beliefs prevented them from doing so. The experiences of participating in daily religious routine in school made Justine believe that she would do the same when she moved to the United States. However, she was taken aback on her first day at school in the United States, to learn that there would not ever be any morning prayer or even religious education classes at her public school since such religious activities conflicted with the law. Justine met a student who, like herself, was new to the school, but whose Muslim faith made him accepting of the laws barring daily Christian devotions in public schools.

Throughout the years, court cases have addressed whether or not religion should be taught in schools. Wiggins (2009) mentions that in 1940, members of different faiths in Champaign, Illinois formed the group named Champaign Council on Religious Education. During public school hours, the group offered voluntary religious instruction to students. Students who did not want to receive religious studies were sent to another classroom to continue their secular studies. The Court found that the use of tax-supported property for religious instruction violated the establishment clause. This action was considered to be special treatment for students to receive religious education instead of secular education, and it was therefore unconstitutional. In another case, the Board of Regents for New York State authorized a short prayer at the start of each school day (Wiggins, 2009). At its simplest form, the invocations acknowledged God and people's dependence on Him, and asked for His blessings. The prayer is non-denominational because it only invokes God's name. Nonetheless, the court found the prayer unconstitutional because by providing the prayer, New York officially approved religion. This case was another attempt to eliminate prayer from school. A third case involved Engel versus Vitale, (1962), when parents of different faith residing in New York sued because they did not want their children subjected to recite a prayer written by a New York education board (Wiggins, 2009). The courts agreed with the parents. Furthermore, in Abington Township School District versus Schempp (1963), the Supreme Court ruled that sponsoring Bible readings and reciting the Lord's Prayer were unconstitutional. The fight against religion in schools continued in the Pennsylvania public schools. Each day would begin with students reading at least ten verses from the Bible. After the reading, the students would recite the Lord's Prayer. Of course, students could be excused from any of the religious practices with a written note from their parents. The court concluded that the required religious practices were unconstitutional. In addition, although a parent could write a note to excuse his or her child from these religious activities, it was irrelevant since the school was violating the establishment clause. Nowadays, if parents prefer for their children to learn about the family's religious faith, then they have the option of enrolling their child in a private school that includes prayer and religious classes within the institution's curriculum.

Misconceptions on prayer in public schools have resulted in various violations of the law by some school districts that initially implemented religious restrictions such as forbidding students to carry a Bible to school or even wear a religious T-shirt. Under the United States Constitution, prayer is a protected form of free speech. As an individual, a student may pray in various areas of the school or at a student run Bible club (Anti-Defamation League, 2013). They may pray silently prior to or after the instructional periods. Students may say a blessing before eating their meal. Students may also engage with each other in religious activity when classes are not in session. Students are also not prevented from speaking about religious topics with their peers but should not engage in religious harassment that causes disruption of a class. Such personal religious activities of students will meet the guidelines of the law only if they are not coerced or supervised or endorsed by school officials or staff. Since a diverse population is enrolled in many public schools, it is important that the public schools respect the religious beliefs of all students. Nevertheless, some schools continue to misread the law. For instance, in 2004, a Colorado high school banned a group of students who wanted to pray, sing Christian songs, and discuss religious topics during their free time in an unoccupied choir room.

Justine was relieved to know that while prayer conducted by school personnel is outlawed, there is no law against engaging in individual, silent, personal prayers in public schools. This type of personal prayer should not cause any disruption to the school's education schedule (Anti-Defamation League, 2013). Additional report on the prayer in school laws may be obtained at **http://archive.adl.org/religion_ps_2004/prayer.html#.VezvXBFV ikp**

Overseas Teachers Wanted ...For Failing Schools

Yolanda was excited when she heard the news on Monday morning from other teachers at her school. They were all discussing an announcement in the newspaper that a private company from the United States would be in town during the next couple of weeks to recruit teachers to work in that country. For not only Yolanda, but many of her colleagues, this would be an opportunity of a lifetime to migrate and work legally in the United States at their chosen profession. So, as with many other teachers in her country, Yolanda thought all day about applying for a teaching position in the United States. She was impressed the recruitment agency would be responsible for all immigrant services, including H-1B visas for six years and adjustments to green cards. The agency offered educational services such as assisting teachers to obtain state certification. Furthermore, she was even more pleased to know that her family would be able to migrate with her. For such promises of living a good life with added financial benefits, Yolanda applied. But, during the process, the recruiters charged a fee for every step of the application, so it turned out to be more than she bargained for. The required high fees for placement caused her to be in debt to family members and friends. Nevertheless, Yolanda was still optimistic about the application. She was overjoyed when she was notified of her acceptance to teach in the United States.

Some school districts in the United States are unwilling or unable to address the root causes of teacher shortage. Instead, they try to fix the issue by hiring overseas-trained teachers. By 2007, 19,000 foreign born teachers were working in the United States on temporary visas and the number continues to increase steadily (USA Today, 2008). Yolanda was now included in this number of teachers. Yolanda was grateful that she was not thrown into the classroom immediately since an orientation and workshops were organized to enable the recruits to become familiar with teaching in the United States. However, she was overwhelmed with different issues upon arrival. One of the most troubling issue for her was that she was placed in a middle school in an inner-city community to teach students with developmental and behavioral problems. Yolanda was not used to such an environment since she had taught for many years at a school where students showed discipline and respected teachers. During her first week of teaching, she did not understand how students could be so disrespectful to anyone in authority. There were also metal detectors to curve any student's attempt to take a weapon inside the school building; parents came to the school to challenge teachers; and she experienced other situations that she was not accustomed me. During the first semester, Yolanda remembers crying almost every day on arrival home. Many times, she wondered if it would be a better option for her to return to her native country. Many teachers struggle with the different challenges they have to face. According to the American Federation of Teachers (2009), overseas teachers are being placed primarily in hard-to-staff inner-city or very rural schools teaching the hard-to-fill disciplines of math, science, and special education. In addition, many school districts have trouble retaining teachers for reasons that include low pay, disruptive students, and a lack of books and materials (USA Today, 2008). Further, students tend to show resistance when they are distracted by the unfamiliar accents of the overseas-teachers even though they may be speaking perfect English, their native language. In that regard, the students will also make fun of how the teacher speaks which can become annoying. So, when overseas teachers come to the United States, they have to learn about the American culture, urban culture, the poverty and challenges of children living in inner-city communities.

Moreover, the contract was not what it had initially appeared to be. Yolanda and others believed that they were lured to the United States with promises of better-paying jobs, improved educational opportunities, housing assistance, and the path to permanent residency. Yet, ten years later, the promises of permanent residency did not materialize. In the meantime, due to Yolanda's immigration status, her daughter was considered an international student and required to pay the exorbitant college fees which Yolanda could not afford.

In 2011, nearly 1,050 foreign teachers were caught in the middle of a workplace dispute between the Prince George's County Public Schools and the United States Labor Department (Leitsinger, 2011).

After settling their mishandling of the H-1B Visa program with the Labor Department, the school district notified foreign teachers that the school district could not rehire them when their visas expired. Of course, the news threw the teachers' lives into disarray as they frantically searched for other jobs across the country although they could not legally work in the United States without a sponsor. The situation left a financial and emotional burden on the teachers.

Some of the other issues that foreign recruited teachers complain about include: finding out that they are unable to participate in the pension plan, so they are not provided any insurance coverage except for possibly, dental; paying high rent even when they are initially housed in dormitories where they have to sleep on bunk beds; having to fend for themselves to make their own housing arrangements after two weeks of arrival; rent is not subsidized, so they face high costs each month. In fact, the recruiters require teachers to pay for so many services that some can barely survive on the monies that they receive bi-weekly after these deductions are made. Yolanda was recruited from a pool of teachers that were considered the best and brightest teachers. Yet, her experiences as an overseas teacher made her wonder if she had made the wrong decision. Upfront information from recruiters would certainly have made her think twice. The following website includes reports on the causes and consequences of international teacher recruitment - **http://www.aft.org/sites/default/files/wysiwyg/importingeducators0609.pdf**

College Athletes' Illiteracy Cover-Up

Amir excelled as an overall athlete in various sports in his country. But, playing a sport certainly could not interfere with his parents' expectation that their child still had to work hard to attain good grades. Therefore, his upbringing taught him that a student is not only expected to excel in a chosen sport but also in the classroom. This high expectation was embedded in Amir when he gained a track scholarship to a university located in the United States. There, he devoted many hours to training and also made the same effort to pass his classes. However, Amir realized that his devotion to succeeding in school was not the common reaction to learning by many of the student athletes who were involved in the popular sports on campus. He was aware that a professional athletic career is not a guarantee, so he would need to obtain a degree that could allow him to establish a stable career.

Since education was always instilled as number one rather than athletic abilities, Amir was surprised that in the United States, illiteracy seemed to be common among male student athletes such as those who play popular sports. These promising male student athletes are highly recruited from high schools by college scouts. However, more emphasis is placed on the students' athletic abilities rather than their education. For some of these athletes, the learning process has been difficult for them throughout their lives and such issues often leave many with the inability to read or write at a satisfactory grade level. Yet, they still are allowed to enter college based on their athletic abilities. For many of these students, sports rather than education has been their outlet to shine. Furthermore, these young men see others like themselves from similar economic and social backgrounds who have achieved stardom and riches from playing professional sports. So, education takes a backseat to building their athletic aspirations. These star struck students do not realize that many of these professional athletes, like themselves, are illiterate. Nevertheless, athletic recruiters bombard and try to lure high school star athletes to play for their colleges. The recruitment efforts are generally not in the best interest of these athletes since the main purpose is to recruit without giving any consideration to learning issues. Amir heard on the news that some National Collegiate Athletic Association (NCAA) institutions try to cover up their student's illiteracy by having work/study students or tutors complete an athlete's work.

One publicized case is the University of North Caroline where a tutor panicked when she realized that some student athletes who she was assigned to teach could not read, yet they were participating in multi-million dollar producing sports. To make matters worse for these athletes, for approximately 18 years, University of North Caroline – Chapel Hill appeared to be involved in a system of no-show classes that were encouraged by academic counselors for the athletes. The pride of winning games created the long standing cover-up of athletes' lack of ability to successfully complete classes on their own merit. According to Kane and Stancil (2014) lecture-style classes were somehow converted into fake independent studies to keep struggling athletes eligible to continue participating in their sport. An eight month investigation uncovered that class counselors sent student athletes to bogus courses that expected them to only turn in papers rather than attend classes. Investigations uncovered that the cheating fiasco was widespread and well-coordinated with athletic officials knowing how their players were obtaining better grades, but their winning desire overtook the need to stop this fiasco. In the long run, many athletes over the past 18 years failed to establish a professional athletic career or obtain the education to secure a working career.

One example of the incompetence which currently prevails at many schools involves a former running back whose course load included courses such as bowling, billiards and watercolor painting. He lost his eligibility when it was discovered that he was obtaining too much assistance with his papers. However, he filed a federal lawsuit which mentioned that the university broke their promise by failing to provide him with an education in return for playing sports. So, he indicates that the university did not keep him on the right academic track because the main focus was athletics rather than education (Ganim, 2014).

Amir knows that the University of North Carolina's issue is not isolated as this disservice to student athletes is widespread in a multi-million dollar sports industry. Nevertheless, Amir is pleased that his learning foundation from his native country allowed him to not rely on athletics but, through education, establish the basis for a rewarding work career for his future. The following website takes an in-depth look into the issues with college athletes and provides suggestions to address the illiteracy problems.
http://www.law.seattleu.edu/Documents/sjsj/2012fall/Gatmen.pdf

College Campus Distractions

It was a dream for Aabha to obtain a scholarship to attend a university in the United States. She had successfully completed the Scholastic Achievement Test (SAT), and her high scores opened doors to a number of university offers in the United States. She could not wait to arrive at her chosen university since she continuously thought about living in a different country on her own, meeting other students, and devoting her time to studying. When she arrived at the university, she encountered a busy atmosphere. Aabha saw so many students, like herself, checking into their dormitories while others were walking about from one place to the next. After settling in during the first week, Aabha realized that she chose a university where it was the custom for students to attend football and basketball games to support the teams. She learned that both were multi-million dollar sports that brought recognition to institutions. In fact, she found out that many higher education institutions are recognized by their football and basketball teams more so than their academic successes. So, it is beneficial for institutions to have football and basketball teams. Further, Aabha found out that having football and basketball programs also generate millions of dollars for other areas of campus life. For example, successful football and basketball programs affect high enrollment applications. The sale of football and basketball merchandise with the school's logo produces millions, and it is easier for the Board of Trustees to raise money to construct new buildings. However, the irony for Aabha was that athletes have generated so much money for universities, but they do not get paid besides obtaining scholarships. As a result, she determined there has been an unbalanced financial system throughout the university sports culture.

Aabha realized that some students paid more attention to not only going to football and basketball games but also going to almost every party on or off campus. It was more alarming to hear her peers brag about how much alcohol they consumed at on-campus or off-campus parties and make jokes about getting drunk to the extent that they could not remember their actions. She decided that such college activities would be a distraction to her. She was there to get an education, and she would not allow such activities to affect her studies.

Another event that was new to Aabha was the sorority and fraternity pledging rituals of students. The comradery of belonging to a group of liked minds was understandable to her, so she wanted to pledge with one of these sororities. However, her feelings quickly changed when she learned horror stories of hazing rituals that some pledgees would have to complete to be considered a part of the group. In addition, Aabha learned that some of the pledgees' rituals at some institutions were so outrageous and horrible that pledgees suffered severe harm or even death. She found out that in one case at a Florida institution, a pledgee was beaten on a bus so severely that he died. She was told that the female sororities were no better than the male fraternities since the tasks assigned to pledgees were just as severe.

The next issue that caused some concern for Aabha was the knowledge that crimes had occurred on campus. She did not expect to hear this news since she saw the campus police constantly patrolling the institution. In fact, according to United States News Report, while crimes occur on campuses, the response from the universities are significantly underreported because the institutions contend that their reputation would be at stake. The news made her afraid for her safety, so she took precautions by always walking with others after her night classes or when she stayed late at the library. But, what was more disturbing for Aabha was hearing that her university was under investigation by the Federal government for the improper responses to rape reports. She realized that date rape was a major issue not only at her university but others throughout the nation. According to Vedantam (2016), report analysis suggests that rape increases 41% at college football home games. Aabha believes that the consumption of alcohol had gotten out-of-hand and such heavy drinking has placed female students in a vulnerable position where they can easily be taken advantage of. While she was not fond of going to bars and drinking alcohol, Aabha still decided to take precautions so that she would not be one of the victims of crime at her university. Campus safety and security data may be reviewed at **http://ope.ed.gov/security/**

Non-transferable College Credits

When Maurice came to the United States, he saw so many college advertisements on television. He knew that he wanted to pursue a career in health services. However, there were too many schools to choose from. He finally decided to contact two of these institutions after watching their television ads. An immediate enrollment was guaranteed from both for-profit institutions. He did not know that the process would be so easy since he did not have his high school diploma to show proof that he had graduated. That did not seem to be a requirement for acceptance into both of the colleges. He wanted to begin an academic program as soon as possible, so he did not stop to consider that the courses at both institutions were costly. He was even more convinced that he was on his way to achieving his educational goal when he was approved for financial aid.

There were about five students enrolled in Maurice's evening class, but this low enrollment did not bother him since he expected to receive more teacher interaction with less students. The five weeks only class length was a problem, however, as he did not think he could learn enough in such short spaces of time. The standard semester system of approximately 15 weeks are replaced at some of the for-profit colleges with four to five week sessions where lessons are packed into the short period of time. Nevertheless, Maurice continued the program in anticipation of obtaining a Bachelor's degree. After one year, Maurice was no longer satisfied with the program and made a decision to transfer to the local community college where there appeared to be a better administered program at a lower cost. He had also learned that the for-profit college was not placing students in jobs upon graduation, and this was contrary to the admissions counselor's statement when he applied at the school. Maurice was upset with himself for not considering the community college in the first place. However, the enticements of the advertised college and quick, effortless acceptance lured him in.

Maurice completed an application for the community college and submitted it along with a copy of his transcript from the for-profit college. He was disappointed, however, to learn that while the community college would consider his application, none of the credits that he attained during the year at the for-profit college would be accepted for transfer. He tried to dispute the policy but made no headway in convincing the college to accept all credits. He also contacted other public colleges in nearby counties but received the same response or that he could transfer only three credits from one class completed at his last college. His only option was to begin the program from scratch at the community college. Maurice was disappointed since he was in debt for classes that did not seem to meet the standards of state colleges and universities.

When searching for a university to complete higher education courses, it is important to thoroughly research the institution. Not all institutions that carry the name "college" or "university" are guided by the same standards instituted by accreditation agencies. Some of these institutions are known as proprietary schools or for-profit institutions. These new-types of colleges and universities do not have standards for enrollment that are similar to the well-established colleges and universities. For instance, SAT or ACT tests are generally not an enrollment requirement, and neither are satisfactory completion of high school standardized tests considered as essential for enrolling students. Furthermore, some of these proprietary institutions may even enroll students who have not achieved a high school diploma. English language limitations do not prevent acceptance to these colleges. Once any student qualifies for financial aid, such income generating funds guarantee an automatic entry into the institution.

Many of the for-profit colleges have been luring military veterans to enroll. These veterans are a good target since the new G.I. Bill provides service members with subsidies to pursue higher education. A veteran can receive tens of thousands of dollars towards a school of their choice. Underhand marketing tactic includes a for-profit institution illegally using the official seals of the United States military branches in its advertisements to attract recently discharged service men and women.

These institutions engage in advertisement through various medium, so it is difficult not to notice them as Maurice did. While students may not encounter any difficulties in enrolling in such colleges, there are many questions for them to consider before making any decisions. Vasquez (2015) suggests that students should ask enrollment counselors the following questions:

- Do you have accreditation for this program? An accreditation would be considered a gold seal of approval from experts in the field of study. If a student completes a non-accredited program especially in the medical area, they may experience difficulties finding a job.

- What is the total cost of the program?

- Can I take the application documents home and review it? Can I call you back next week? Since the for-profit colleges are so expensive, it is best to do research by reviewing the documents carefully and reading online reviews of the college.

- Does the community college offer the same program? More times than not, the community college will offer the same program at a much cheaper cost. Furthermore, there will be no difficulties in transferring credits accumulated at a community college to a four year university.

- Are you regionally accredited? Most career colleges do not have regional accreditation and therefore the credits will not be transferable to a traditional school.

- If something goes wrong who should I contact? Complaints may be filed with the state's Commission for Independent Education, the state's Attorney General, or the Federal Consumer Financial Protection Bureau (CFPB) when students feel they have been misled.

To file a complaint with the Commission for Independent Education, go to website: **http://bit.ly/1JgUiSD**.   For the Attorney General, see: **http://bit.ly/1QosduG**. The CFPB accepts student loan complaints at: **http://1.usa.gov/1EvFdeN**

DREAMers' Dilemma

Anna arrived in the United States at the tender age of two years old. For almost her entire life, she did not experience any difficulties living in the United States although her mother made her aware that both of them were not legally residing in the United States. Her mother came to the United States with Anna on a Visitor's visa, got a job cleaning houses, and decided not to return to her native country because she wanted her daughter to receive the opportunities that the country has to offer. Anna had achieved excellent grades throughout her time in school. Under normal circumstances, her top performances would have allowed her to gain financial assistance to continue her studies at her preferred university. However, since she was not considered a legal resident, she did not qualify for Federal student loans.

"DREAMers" like Anna have spent their lives in the United States. They are not familiar with their native countries since they left as babies or toddlers. Many consider English as their first language. Anna and others like herself are called DREAMers because of a proposed legislation to offer them immigration status known as the Development, Relief, and Education for Alien Minors (DREAM) Act. These DREAMers graduate from high school to an uncertain future. They are unable to legally work and receive Federal Financial Aid to pursue their educational and economic goals. They may even be deported to their native countries that are unknown to them since they left at young ages. Gonzales (2010) informs that the DREAM Act is a Federal bill that is expected to provide immigration relief to such young people. The passage of the bill would grant them legal residency and Federal Financial Aid. Until Congress passes the DREAM Act, these young people are subject to the same immigration laws as those who have entered the United States as adults. In June, 2012, President Obama's administration announced that it would accept requests for Deferred Action for Childhood Arrivals (DACA). This initiative was implemented to temporarily suspend the deportation of young people who were brought to the United States illegally by their parents. However, these young people must meet certain educational requirements and the criteria established under the legislative proposals such as the DREAM Act. The requirements include that the unauthorized immigrants must be under the age of 31 years; entered the United States before the age of 16 years; have lived in the United States for a minimum of five years; have not been convicted of a crime; a high school graduate or GED recipient; and currently enrolled in school or served in the military.

The Deferred Action to Unauthorized Immigrants is expected to provide economic benefits to an estimated 1.4 million children and young adults (Immigration Council, 2012). Each year, it is speculated that tens of thousands of DREAMers graduate from high school and are often in limbo due to a lack of legal status which prevents them from attending college or working legally. Therefore, these future career professionals now have an opportunity to make the most of their abilities and thereby contribute to the United States' economy.

Congress placed the Dream Act bill on the back burner without any indication that the matter will be re-visited in the future. However, in the meantime, the Dream Act Foundation has partnered with a significant number of learning institutions so that scholarships may be awarded to young adults in order for them to achieve their education goals. Many institutions, including recognizable ones, realized the need to take up the challenge to serve these students (Sheehy, 2014). Also, many states have even allowed these undocumented young people to pay in-state tuition rates at public colleges and universities as long as they meet the requirements. For more information on the DREAMers, see **www.thedream.us**

Chapter 3

Cultural Differences

Stars Wanted - No Talent Required

Gabriella comes from a country where being famous must be earned through recognition of outstanding performances in education, a career, or other accomplishments in areas such as sports, entertainment, etc. Whatever the area, a well-known personality becomes respected for their expertise in a chosen area due to hard work. However, she noticed that becoming famous and even rich in the United States may develop from becoming notorious for displaying bad behavior on videos, being discovered on social media, or participating on a reality show. No effort, education, or other accomplishments seem to be necessary to be considered a "celebrity" in the United States.

Gabriella recognizes that Justin Beiber, became popular and subsequently rich after posting a video on You-Tube. But, she realizes that Beiber has become a media sensation throughout the years not for his musical talents but rather for his consistent bad behavior. In fact, she wondered why after Beiber was arrested on Miami Beach, his story was the number one news in South Florida and other cities. Other more important news took a back seat that day to focus on the arrest. She believes that there are too many entertainment programs that already focus on such issues, so the evening news should not have diverted from its serious format to focus on entertainment news. While it is expected that celebrity magazines and entertainment news programs are going to focus on the private lives of celebrities, one does not turn on the local news expecting for it to be dominated by celebrity news (Wilkerson, 2011).

Gabriella knows that while Beiber has the ability to sing, she has noticed that others aspiring for fame by way of the realty shows display little or no talent. She has seen some realty show participants demonstrating behavior such as: (a) lying or cheating or back stabbing each other in an effort to win the cash jackpot; (b) women engaging in fist fights and other un-ladylike behavior; (c) excessive drinking and bar brawls; (d) teenage mothers displaying a lack of self-respect; (e) promiscuous sex and other behavior that is promoted by the show's producers based on audience ratings.

According to Wilkerson (2011), it appears that everyone wants to be a celebrity nowadays, and this desire is understandable when people such as Paris Hilton and Kim Kardashian have been earning a fortune from doing nothing. Audiences are attracted by an upsurge of reality programs that offer ordinary people the opportunity to become famous. In addition, a bombardment of celebrity coverage by the media has influenced people's aspiration to become famous. Everybody expects to receive something for nothing so becoming a celebrity seems the best route to become rich and famous (Wilkerson, 2011).

Unfortunately, the get rich and famous mentality has negatively affected many teenagers who are growing up with the belief that all they need to do is appear on a reality show to achieve their 15 minutes of fame (Wilkerson, 2011). So, the youth no longer desire to become doctors, lawyers, engineers, etc., but they would rather hope to become pop stars, even if they are unable to sing or dance. The youth is captivated by the glamorous, effortless, fun life of celebrities as seen on television, in magazines, and on the Internet. Landau (2009) cites that a 2006 survey from the Pew Research Center found that 51 percent of 18 – 25 years old responded that being famous was either the first or second most important life goals for their generation. More information on the drive to become a celebrity may be found on **http://www.cnn.com/2009/HEALTH/10/28/psychology.fame.cele brity/**

Proud To Be Arrested

In some foreign countries, such as Xiomara's, there is a stigma if someone is incarcerated since that person is said to have brought shame to his or her family. The family will have to bear the burden of this shame for many years because it is never forgotten among people living in the same community. In such environment, whenever the incarcerated person is released from jail or prison, he or she is never seen again in that community as the family will do all that is possible to send him or her away out of the scrutiny of the neighbors because he or she has been branded for life as a criminal.

In addition, the prisons in Xiomara's country are in deplorable conditions. Inmates have to live in a filthy environment that includes too many inmates housed inside the same cell. These living conditions are further impacted by physical and sexual abuses which are common throughout a corrupt prison system. While the meals are inedible, inmates have no other choice but to eat whatever they are fed. `

Shortly after Xiomara moved to the United States, she was unfamiliar with a bus route and missed her stop. While trying to find the best route to get back to her intended destination, she asked a man for directions. To her surprise, the man showed a disinterest in answering her question by responding loudly that he had just been released from jail and did not know where he himself was going. Xiomara wondered why anyone would choose to make known that they were in jail since this was not good news to brag about in the environment that she grew up. However, she later realized that in the United States, people are not bashful in sharing that they went to jail or prison.

In fact, it did not make sense to Xiomara that in the United States, most former inmates experience some incidents of fear or anxiety after their release back to society, so they may commit offenses in order to get arrested and sent back to jail. An example of the revolving door occurred when former Bexar County Jail inmates sometimes deliberately commit minor crimes so that they will get arrested and return to jail to get their three square meals and a roof over their heads when things get tough on the outside. Further, Ulloa (2011) mentions that these men generally have low levels of education, few job skills, and high incidences of mental health along with substance-abuse issues. Many return to their former dismal life of having no money or family and struggle to find affordable housing and social services. Ulloa (2011) refers to reports that more than four out of ten adult offenders nationwide return to state prisons within three years of their release.

On PBS's Front Line documentary, *Who's Locked Up in America*, a 14 year old girl expressed that she has been locked up on a number of occasions because of her violent temper, and at one point she faced 11 charges. This young lady bragged that her mother, father, brothers, sisters, aunts, uncles, etc. have all been incarcerated a number of times. Unfortunately, incarceration is a never ending cycle for many families. The documentary addressed the fact that 2.3 million persons have been incarcerated for non-violent crimes.

Xiomara later enrolled in a practical nursing program at a vocational school. She mingled with the diverse student population and quickly adapted to attending school in the United States. One issue that she noticed that was unusual to her was a couple of students came to school with a tracking monitor attached to their ankle. She learned from a classmate that the electronic device meant that the wearer had been arrested for committing a misdemeanor and, instead of being remanded to jail, he or she was ordered by the judge to wear the ankle monitor to restrict their movements. Nevertheless, Xiomara could not believe how the ankle monitor was displayed with no shame of the circumstances why the electronic device was attacked to an ankle. In fact, wearing the monitor did not stop female students from wearing shorts or skirts instead of pants to hide the box. It was worn with pride, and this made Xiomara wonder why.

Furthermore, celebrities seem to be jumping on the band wagon since their arrests have become common news. Incidentally, celebrities have made sure they strike a pose for their mug shots so that the photos will appear as a beautiful portrait when they are shown on entertainment and daily news television programs. Their mug shots are also displayed on websites created primarily to show celebrity mugshot images. The following website includes information on inmates who cannot adjust to living outside prison and commit crimes to return to a life they consider safer: **http://www.mysanantonio.com/news/local_news/article/Convictc ouldn-thandlebeing-free-2187648.php**

Alcohol Addiction

A bar could be found at practically every corner of Pauline's town, and her mother owned one of them. Pauline remembers that it was common for some middle age and older men to visit her mother's bar. Going to bars was routine for those men and others especially on Fridays after receiving their paychecks. From time to time a woman would be seen in the company of a man inside a bar, but it was rare to see women in bars except for the bar maid. Moreover, it was not a normal practice for students from high schools, colleges, or universities to frequent bars, consume alcohol, get drunk at parties or at other events. Her over-protective mother did not allow her to go inside their own bar. Anyway, Pauline did not mind because she never cared for the taste of alcohol and disliked watching the out-of-control behavior of a drunk person.

Living in the United States, however, Pauline found the culture of consuming alcohol was different from what she was accustomed to seeing. Pauline observed that in the United States, a variety of people frequented bars. In fact, she felt out of place when she attended college in the United States since it appeared that students were expected to drink alcohol and she did not. As a result, she was often left out of receiving invitations to join her roommates to hang out. She could not believe the peer pressure that existed causing those students, who originally may not have consumed alcohol, to now develop an addiction.

Alcohol use by youth aged 21 years old and below is a major public health problem (Center for Disease Control, 2014). Alcohol is considered the most commonly used and abused drug among youth in the United States. In fact, alcohol is used more than tobacco and illicit drugs. According to the Center for Disease Control (2014): (a) alcohol is responsible for more than 4,300 annual deaths among underage youth; (b) although drinking by persons under the age of 21 is illegal, people aged 12 to 20 years drink 11% of all alcohol consumed in the United States; (c) Binge drinking represents more than 90% of the alcohol consumed; (d) on average, underage drinkers consume more drinks per drinking occasion than adult drinkers; (e) in 2010, there were approximately 189,000 emergency rooms visits by persons under age 21 for injuries and other conditions linked to alcohol.

The binge drinking of college students has become an epidemic. According to the National Institute of Alcohol Abuse (2013), college drinking is a significant public health problem, and the misuse and underage drinking take an enormous toll on the academic and social lives of students on campuses across the United States. Research shows that more than 80 percent of college students drink alcohol, and almost half report binge drinking in the past 2 weeks. In fact, 1,825 college students between the ages of 18 and 24 die each year from alcohol-related unintentional injuries. Drinking at colleges has become such a ritual that students often regard drinking as a necessary part of their higher education experience. Many students have already established their drinking habits prior to attending a college, so the college environment can exacerbate the existing problem. Unfortunately, practically all college students experience the effects of college drinking—whether they drink or not.

Alcohol abuse is even prevalent among soccer moms. Dennis & Braiker (2009) report that an untold number of mothers is considered closet alcoholics. These women have developed serious drinking problems due to the stresses of motherhood and other family problems. While apparently there are no statistics on the number of alcoholic moms, high profile tragedies have highlighted the topic. One such tragedy that Pauline remembers occurred when a mother driving under the influence of alcohol in the wrong direction on the Taconic State Parkway, NY, collided head-on with an oncoming SUV. The driver's daughter, three nieces, and three passengers in the SUV died. It is also disturbing to Pauline that, within seven months in 2014, three Broward County, Florida judges were arrested and charged with driving while under the influence of alcohol. For facts on alcohol related cases, statistics, state laws, etc., see **http://www.madd.org/statistics/?referrer=https://www.google.com/**

What's in a Taste?

"I miss the food from my country!" "The food doesn't taste the same...it has an unnatural taste!" Auguste and other immigrants have voiced these complaints when asked about how they are adjusting to eating certain American food. Auguste now resides in a city where he can easily obtain many of the foods that he is accustomed to eating in his native land. However, he believes that the meats and land gown food in his country have a different taste – in fact, a better taste when cooked. He thinks that too much fertilizer and other practices are used in the United States to achieve rapid growth of food and animals, and such methods have negatively impacted the food's quality and taste. So, while Auguste and other immigrants purchase the same kinds of food enjoyed in their native land, the differences in taste are noticed. In many developing countries, people are used to purchasing meats, fruits, vegetables, and other land grown products from local community farmers who allow their produces to grow naturally within the expected season. These farmers are not confined to capitalistic expectations for crops to unnaturally ripen and hasten the growth of animals. Instead, it is customary for Auguste to see naturally grown produces in abundance throughout roadside markets and inside supermarkets.

Auguste was made aware that questionable practices occur for the growth of hens. According to Murray (2007) the lighting is manipulated to change the hen's environment and biological cycle. The hens are subjected to long periods of simulated daylight to encourage them to lay outside of the natural cycle. Further, an additional laying cycle may be created when the hens endure a period of darkness. During such period, the hen has been placed on a reduced or starvation diet. The overcrowded environment has restricted movements in the confined cages. Egg-laying hens under-go genetic manipulation too because they are bred to produce high egg volume.

In addition, the American Society for the Prevention of Cruelty to Animals (ASPCA) reports that meat chickens are grown over three times faster than those during pre-World War II. In addition, while chickens may live as long as up to 10 years, the factory hens are usually killed by six weeks old. These meat chickens are bred for maximum breast meat.

It was alarming for Auguste to also know that questionable practices extend to cattle. Calves no longer grow to maturity at a natural pace thereby reaching two to three years of age (Robinson, 2008). Instead, cattle are brought to slaughter weight within one to two years. As a result, the nutritional value of the meat is affected. Consumers are more at risk from bacterial contamination; and consumers are exposed to a number of unwanted chemicals. While hamburger meat may look fresh, the deep red color indicates that it is injected with gasses and the juiciness may be enhanced by water, salt, preservatives and other additives. Therefore, Robinson (2008) notes that consumers should be aware of the traces of hormones, antibiotics and other chemicals that were not produced by the cow.

Food that is free of pesticides, hormones, and antibiotics may be purchased in specialty food stores or those products may be found stocked at major grocery chain stores. The need for organic food is due to the popular demand of many who prefer consuming chemical free products. However, food free of synthetic ingredients cost approximately 20 to 100 percent more than the chemically produced equivalent (Valliant, 2014). The cost is affected by factors such as: (a) increase labor costs; (b) the demand overrules the supply; (c) fertilizer cost is higher; (d) rotation of crop is necessary; and (e) smaller shipments are expected. The U.S. Food and Drug Administration's website, **http://www.hhs.gov/healthcare/rights/**, provides information on the regulations governing the food industry

Humanizing Pets

Anil did not have a pet while growing up as a child, so he never felt comfortable around animals. Furthermore, years ago in his country, dogs were kept outside of the house for protection and not allowed inside. However, nowadays, he notices that the culture has changed because more natives are bonding with their animals and keeping them inside their homes. Anil thought that this new found bonding with pets was the best treatment that any animal could receive. But, his thinking was surpassed by the lavish treatment he noticed was given to pets in the United States by their owners. He saw that some pets were fed only organic foods and groomed finely. Anil was also intrigued by the availability of pet hotels, resorts, and that pets are even left as the primary beneficiaries on their owner's Last Will and Testament. Dogs are paraded in dog shows and treated more like extremely spoiled children as opposed to anything else. He recognizes that many owners try to make their pets seem more human in many instances that include: dressing them in clothes to mimic human wear, taking them shopping for groceries, comforting them in strollers, purchasing high cost furniture, and laying them to rest in pet cemeteries. Anil believes that those who treat their animals as humans are quite aware that their dogs do not know or care to be treated as such. But, he surmises that such behavior of an owner is a way of serving the owner's desires instead of the best interest of the pet.

Unfortunately, domestic animals nowadays depict how nature works. Anil recognizes that by having dogs or any kind of pet, owners become accustomed to seeing animals behave calmly and have no fear. However, Anil refuses to let down his guard around animals since he believes it is very easy to forget that most animals do not trust people or can be domesticated. There are reports of vicious mauling or death of those who have climbed into confined areas at zoos in order to interact with animals, not understanding that those animals do not trust human behaviors. Fatal cases of animal attacks have also taken place in homes. In Miami-Dade County, a 4-year boy was mauled to death by a family pet dog (Burke, 2014). This situation is all too common throughout the United States. During

2013, there were 32 dog bite related fatalities, and pit bulls accounted for 78% (25) of the deaths (dogbite.org, 2014). Yet, many do not believe that dog breeds such as pit bulls create danger to anyone.

Anil certainly understands how dogs can serve a purpose and need to be house bread. Visual impairment and some medical conditions require the need for dogs as companionship. However, cases where some take in more dogs and cats in their household than they can handle have caused an unhealthy way of life. The current year is no different from other years when people rescued more animals than they could control. For instance in Orlando, a couple lived with their two small children in a house of filth that was soiled with animal waste from 15 pit bulls that were infested with insects. More than 100 animals were removed from a filthy Buffalo house of a 70 year old woman. Over 100 animals were found in a Long Island home while the woman was being evicted. In response to a complaint, Parma animal control officers found over 200 animals living under deplorable conditions. These incidents indicate that the love for animals may sometimes get out of hand which can develop into a neglect of the animal versus the initial intentions to care for the animal.

Anil also notices that too often owners are negligent in supervising their dogs while walking them. He sees that dog walkers may allow the animals to: (a) defecate on people's property and walkers make no attempt to clean up after them; (b) be unleashed and left to roam on their own even knowing that their dog is unsafe around other animals and people; and c) accidentally get away from them since the animal may be overpowering and they cannot maintain control of the dog's behavior. While Anil lives in an environment that is consumed with animal lovers, he knows he will never establish a close connection with animals. So, he will continue to be on guard when an animal approaches especially when he notices that the dog walker is not in control. Information on laws, animal adoption, and other issues relating to the protection of animals may be found at **http://www.humanesociety.org/about/departments/legislation/sta te_legislation.html?credit=web_globalfooter?referrer=https://w ww.google.com/**

Gentrification

Gentrification is a word that was unknown to Joaquin until he migrated to a city in the United States. He experienced the process of gentrification when commercial developers bought property in his impoverished neighborhood and steadily converted the community by building upscale housing and commercial construction. The positive experience for him and the long-time residents was the revitalization of the community. However, the negative was that the upscale housing and commercial property attracted middle class and wealthy outsiders, and this action caused rents and property values to increase. The increases resulted in the displacement of many including Joaquin who could no longer afford to live in the neighborhood since his rent was not controlled. So, the bottom-line for Joaquin was that the new construction, influx of resources, and the increased financial activity were not beneficial because they were not enjoyed by the original residents who had to move to less expensive neighborhoods. Joaquin saw this as a social injustice in which wealthy White people were praised for saving the neighborhood.

Joaquin learned that gentrification was a common practice since residents in Harlem, NY experienced similar problems. Goffe (2014) sums it up best when he states that "the hubs of black soul – from barbershops to restaurants – are increasing being whitewashed". Goffe (2014) reports on the history that during the great migration many Blacks from the South moved to Harlem in order to escape racism. Harlem became the mecca for Black culture, and the historic period of music, art, poetry, and theatre became known as the Harlem Renaissance. Harlem not only attracted southern Blacks, but an influx of people from the West Indies and Puerto Rico arrived during the 1950s. During the 1980s people from West Africa populated the area. The overcrowding atmosphere bread poverty, drugs, and crime for many years (Goffe, 2014). During that period, Whites regarded Harlem as an unsafe place to even drive through. However, gentrification has ended that stigma. Today, the Black population has begun to decline as Whites move into the expensive residences in Harlem. To accommodate this new population, Black bookshops, Caribbean shops, and barber shops are steadily replaced with upscale supermarkets, fancy restaurants, specialty boutiques. Many Blacks remaining in Harlem live below the poverty line. Harlem is not the only area in New York that is prone to gentrification. During the 1960s and 1970s Crown Heights was plagued with poverty, racial conflicts, high rate of unemployment and crime. Developers took over the Franklin Avenue area and built condominiums and commercial property to service the needs of middle class and wealthy residents who moved into the neighborhood. As a result of the rising rental prices, long-time residents on Franklin Avenue have been moving away. However, Crown Heights remains an overall ethnic and social combination where a wide variety of people from older residents to new immigrants and other groups continue to reside.

Further, in speaking to a co-worker, Joaquin was informed that gentrification also transformed the Mission District in San Francisco. The district was established during the 1940s to 1960s when an influx of Mexican immigrants moved into the area. The domination of Latino residence continued throughout the 1960's when immigrants from Central America called the Mission district their home. Businesses catering to the Latino market served the vibrant population. However, during the 1990s, the dot.com boom attracted young technology personnel into the district, and the immigrant neighborhood was no longer the same. The drastic increase in commercial rental property resulted in many long standing minority businesses closing. Bodegas were replaced with high-end businesses such as upscale supermarkets and boutiques with specialty products such as organic chocolate. Marketplaces where people gathered to socialize have become cafes where the technology personnel get together. Real estate prices have risen and priced out the original residents who can no longer afford to reside in the area. Some remain in spite of the high rent and housing prices, but the area indicates a drop in the Latino population. The widespread practices of gentrification in the United States occurred also as Black residents in a Columbus, Ohio community fought to restore their beautiful yet run-down community and prevent Whites from taking over the neighborhood.

According to Bryant & Poitras (n.d.) in the PBS documentary, *Flag Wars*, many aspects of the gentrification process are desirable. However, the benefits of these changes are often enjoyed unfairly by the wealthier new arrivals, while the established residents are left out in the cold. Immigrants may probably live in one of the many gentrified neighborhoods where they could hear from a long time resident how a low income population was displaced from the community. As such, gentrification is not restricted to Joaquin's neighborhood or Harlem or San Francisco or Columbus. A developer's greed in purchasing low income properties and displacing its residents is widespread in other communities in states such as Washington D.C., Boston, Chicago, Seattle, and others. Immigrants will come to realize that populations within communities in the United States are not stagnant as some may hope (Bryant & Poitras, n.d.). Circumstances such as gentrification may cause a population to experience displacement from a community that they and their forefathers have lived all their lives. Tips for saving neighborhoods from gentrification may be accessed at **http://www.nytimes.com/roomfordebate/2014/04/13/the-pros-and-cons-of-gentrification/to-save-neighborhoods-get-creative-with-the-law**

Elderly Disconnect

During Natasha's childhood, she always enjoyed visiting her Grandma Annie. She looked forward to helping her grandmother bake or plant flowers or do other fun activities that her grandmother planned for her. In fact, from kindergarten through high school, Natasha usually spent her entire summer holidays with Grandma Annie. As the years passed, while Natasha attended college, she noticed a change in her grandmother's behavior. Her memory seemed to be declining rapidly, and sometimes she appeared to be disoriented. Her family tried to convince Grandma Annie to sell her home and move in with them. However, Grandma Annie stubbornly refused to give up her independence. But, changes to the living conditions were imminent when Grandma Annie left her home one day and could not find her way back. Grandma Annie's unknown whereabouts for several hours made the family aware that it was time to take charge of her welfare. So, she moved to the family home where she could be taken care of rather than living by herself. That is the way it has been in her country - grandparents live with their families who are expected to take care of them.

When Natasha migrated to the United States, she eventually obtained employment at a nursing home. This was an eye-opener for her since many of the elderly residents seemed to have no relatives or friends that would take the time to visit them. It was difficult for Natasha because she came from a background where elderly persons were usually embraced in a son or daughter's family home. But she learned from other co-workers that it was a common practice for people in the United States to abandon their elderly relatives in nursing homes or leave them to live on their own and occasionally visit them.

Natasha realizes that in the United States, some children have to make a difficult choice of looking after their elderly parents at home or place them in a nursing home instead. She wants to believe that most will try their best to accommodate their parents at home. However, far too often at her job, she realizes that some children are given a Power of Attorney for their parents and will pay the nursing home bills from their parent's asset but will make no effort to visit their parents. Natasha has also become aware that in a worst case scenario, some children who have access to their parents' finances may believe that they should pay themselves from their parents' income since they expect to inherit the assets anyway.

Lin (2010) wrote that in the United States, the elderly are typically sent to nursing homes that are often portrayed as delivering uncaring and even cruel treatment to its residents. It is a fact that many societies treat their elderly better than Americans do since other cultures show respect and devotion to the elderly. For example, in the East Asian culture it is considered despicable if children do not take care of their elderly parents. In the Mediterranean cultures, multigenerational families live together in the same house which is a great contrast to the United States where the elderly does not typically live with their children.

There is a disregard for advice or teaching or experience from older people, and this causes a lack of desire to understand their wisdom (Lin, 2010). Therefore, it is no longer common in the United States for families to spend much time with elderly parents. When families are too busy with their own lives, elderly parents may be regarded as another burden, annoying, intrusive rather than a person who can impart knowledge from their years of experience. For information on elderly services and programs, see **http://www.aoa.gov/**

Chapter 4

Social Supportive Services

Resettlement Program

Arriving in the United States for the first time and adjusting to the lifestyle present different experiences for immigrants. Solomon was nervous travelling to the United States for the first time. After disembarking the airplane, he anxiously followed other passengers. Solomon's first impression was the spaciousness of the airport in comparison to his country's airport. He and the other passengers came to a point where they were stopped by Immigration officers accompanied with dogs. The Immigration officers requested for the passengers to present their documents and respond to questions. He heard from another passenger that this was customary only for passengers arriving on flights from certain countries. Getting through that hurdle, he walked a long distance and met up with a crowd of passengers from other flights who were also heading to the immigration processing area. After presenting his documents and clearing immigration, he proceeded to the baggage claims area. Locating his luggage was not the end of the process since Solomon realized that he now had to go through Customs. He went through an area where his luggage was scanned. When the lengthy process was over, Solomon was relieved to finally walk outside to the arrival area where he was met by a family member. As his relative drove home, he was mesmerized by the highways, skyscrapers, and so many enticing, beautifully lit buildings. It was exciting for Solomon to finally arrive in the United States. Solomon's initial arrival went smoothly; however, after settling in, he knew that adapting to his new home would not be easy since his relatives always seemed to be too busy and clueless in directing him where to go and what to do. So, Solomon had to struggle to assimilate into the new society.

Solomon knew, however, that this struggle in adapting to life in the United States was not the same for all immigrants. He wished that he could have eased into society as his neighbor, Lourdes. When she arrived from Cuba, there was a crowd of family members and friends at the airport to welcome her to the country. In addition, a host of social agency services were available to help her learn how to maneuver the system step-by-step. This welcoming process is the same for others who are classified as refugees as a result of their arrival from certain countries. Programs provide reception and resettlement services. These programs are also expected to ensure the well-being and smooth transition of the immigrant to their new life. The immigrants are provided with 30 days of orientation and referral services if they have relatives already residing in the United States. However, if the immigrant does not identify any relatives, the program provides up to 180 days of resettlement services and financial assistance. In addition, programs guarantee the immigrant's financial self-sufficiency through introduction and employment to their new community. Refugee resettlement also includes medical assistance, English language training, and other integration programs. ESL and Adult Education programs, offered by public institutions, generally provide refugee services that include free tuition and books. Other services may enable assistance with enrolling refugee children in schools; finding and furnishing housing prior to refugee arrivals; assisting with public transportation; and familiarizing refugees with shopping for groceries and clothes.

The difference between Solomon's situation and those having refugee status is that they may have arrived through a visa lottery system or they may have stowed away or paid to enter the country via a water vessel. The policy of immigrants, such as those from Cuba, who travel by sea through illegal methods and land on the United States soil is known informally as the "wet foot dry foot" policy. The informal name was given to a 1995 agreement which indicates that Cuban migrants seeking passage to the United States who have been intercepted at sea ("wet foot") are sent back to Cuba or to a third country, while those who make it to United States' soil ("dry foot") are allowed to remain in the country. Immigrants from other countries such as Haiti, however, who come under the same circumstances and land on United States' soil are usually repatriated to their homeland once they are caught entering the country illegally. This treatment has continued to create an outcry of discrimination since some Haitians claim political reprisals will occur if they are returned to their native land.

One community such as Morgan County, Colorado, has established a volunteer group that works on connecting newly arrived immigrants with the nationals. The group uses funding from Colorado Trust to organize English and civics lessons. The group also conducts meetings, organize concerts and food festivals so that the new immigrants may interact with residents of the community. The group provides a drop-in center for immigrants to stop by to discuss how to navigate United States bureaucracy such as the Department of Motor Vehicles, hospitals, school system, etc. Solomon believes resettlement programs should be available in communities throughout the United States for all new immigrants and not be restricted to some groups. For more information on immigrant resettlement agencies, see the following **http://www.acf.hhs.gov/programs/orr/programs**

Facing Homelessness

Jacque was used to seeing poverty and homelessness in his native country and even more so after the devastating earthquake that had left thousands of people dead or without housing. When he moved to the United States, however, he did not expect to see a similar plight of poverty and homelessness in such an influential country. After all, the United States has been known as one of the richest nations in the world. Going downtown, he noticed there were so many homeless people. He saw mostly men, but a few women walking, sitting, or lying along the side walk of a back street. Jacque later learned that the homeless tended to hang out around this block where a shelter with feeding facility is located. There, they receive free breakfast, lunch, and dinner. Since the people receive other services from the facility, it was a favorite hang-out spot for many. Jacque knew that mental illness can keep people from leaving the streets as he often saw in his country. But, he realizes that others seemed to have grown accustomed to their street living and will not leave that life regardless of the aid and opportunities they receive.

A Department of Housing and Urban Development report indicates that in the United States roughly 610,000 homeless people were living in emergency shelters, transitional housing, a decreased or unsheltered locations (Ellis, 2013). However, the National Law Center on Homelessness & Poverty counters that this number excludes millions of Americans who are without housing and living doubled up or in motels because Housing and Urban Development (HUD) programs are full. The report also indicated that student homelessness was on the rise.

In the United States, a National Center on Family Homelessness report includes that 1.6 million children, or one in 45 children, were living on the street, in homeless shelters or motels, or doubled up with other families during 2010 (Bello, 2011). In addition, during 2010, the fastest-growing group of homeless people was women with children. At the First Light Shelter in Birmingham, Alabama, the executive director mentioned that the residence over flows every night since it houses about 125 women and children. Further, after new showing that a majority of students in public schools throughout the American South and West are poor, Strauss (2013) informs that United States public schools are now enrolling over 1.1 million, a record number of homeless children and youth. Data from the United States Department of Education shows that the largest population of these children lives in California, New York, Texas and Florida. Many of the children are very young, so they are in their parents' care. However, others are under-aged teenagers who are on their own on the streets facing the dangers as they struggle to finish high school. Such children who experience homelessness often grow up traumatized by their everyday conditions and may ultimately be affected by chronic health problems (Giraud, 2013). They also may suffer from emotional development.

Jacque was even more disturbed to hear that the homeless included veterans and some of them recently returned from Iraq or Afghanistan. Statistics show that half of the veterans suffer from mental illness and two-thirds suffer from substance abuse problems (Greendoors, n.d.). However, many suffer both mental illness and a substance abuse problem so these have a dual diagnosis. While the Veteran's Administration has provided housing to thousands of veterans, the issue is greater than the federal agency can handle. So, poverty, lack of support networks, and dismal living conditions in overcrowded or substandard housing continue to cause veterans to become homeless. For further information on homelessness and assistance visit **http://nationalhomeless.org/references/need-help/**

Unaffordable Healthcare

It is common to see medical offices for doctors, dentists and optometrists throughout the community where Joshua resided in his native country. In fact, it took less than five minutes to walk from Joshua's house to his doctor's office. As a full time employee, he had insurance that took care of his medical expenses. However, even if he was not working, Joshua did not have to worry since the country's national health insurance was provided to those who could not afford to pay for medical expenses. The problem, however, with national health in his country was the lengthy appointment scheduling periods between doctor's visits and also the long waiting time to see the doctor on the day of an appointment. Joshua and many people in his country accepted this inconvenience since it was still better than not having medical services.

When Joshua arrived in the United States, his goal was to obtain a full time job because it was important for him to have medical insurance and the other benefits. To his surprise, however, while he was fortunate to obtain a full time job, no insurance was offered to the employees at that company. Joshua learned that it was not mandatory for employers hiring a certain number of personnel to provide insurance to their workers. So, Joshua was disappointed to learn that if he got sick, he would be responsible for paying his own medical bills. He could not believe that some developing countries such as his own were offering public health insurance to its needy population yet such an influential, powerful nation such as the United States had no national health insurance in place to address the health concerns of its residents. Even so, those who were lucky to have a job that offered full insurance coverage were burdened with the ever increasing high costs deducted from their paychecks. When Joshua was diagnosed with a medical condition that required surgery, he resorted to returning to his native country for the operation because he determined that the costs would be significantly cheaper.

A Harvard study found that people without health insurance had a 40 percent higher risk of death than those with private health insurance since the uninsured were unable to obtain necessary medical care. The risk appears to have increased since 1993, when a similar study found the threat of death was 25 percent greater for the uninsured. Furthermore, according to Abelson (2009), a Harvard medical study linked the lack of insurance to 45,000 deaths a year in the United States. Additional information indicates that the increase in health risk of the uninsured is likely to be a result of at least two factors. One of these factors is that the uninsured has a greater difficulty in finding care because public hospitals have closed or have cut back on services. The other factor is that medical care has improved for insured people with treatable chronic conditions like high blood pressure. So, as health care for the insured improved, a gap between the insured and uninsured increases.

In 2011, a 24-year-old Cincinnati father died from a tooth infection because he could not afford his medication (Gann, 2011). When dentists told him that his tooth must be pulled, he decided to forgo the procedure because he was unemployed and had no health insurance. He went to the emergency room when his face started swelling, and his head began to ache. He received prescriptions for antibiotics and pain medications. Since the man was unable to afford both, he chose the pain medications. The tooth infection spread and caused his brain to swell.

Joshua was pleased when President Obama made healthcare as one of his priorities and, after much disapproval from the Republicans in Congress, the law passed to provide health insurance to masses of people who needed this important benefit. Even after the technical enrollment difficulties on the implementation of the Affordable Care Act also known as Obamacare, Joshua was overjoyed when he enrolled in a healthcare program since he would now be covered for his pre-existing condition. The Department of Health and Human Services confirms that over 8 million individuals signed up for health insurance during the initial months of its implementation. So, these people now have peace of mind knowing that they have access to insurance. Yet, during a question and answer class discussion with approximately 70 students enrolled in two ESL classes, approximately 98% of the students indicated that they did not qualify for the Affordable Care Act because they were either not employed or the premium was too expensive for them to afford. Also, some Republican governors have resisted taking federal funding to enhance their Medicaid program so as to allow those who do not qualify for the Affordable Care Act to receive other medical benefits. Therefore, while the Affordable Care Act has addressed the needs of millions, far too many are still unable to obtain health benefits. For information on the Affordable Care Act, click on the following **http://www.hhs.gov/healthcare/rights/**

Low Income Housing

Jasmin comes from a country where people who are impoverished are often forgotten. They build their houses from board, zinc, and whatever building scraps they can find. These dilapidated structures are located anywhere vacant land can be found, and the residents remain at these sites, living under deplorable conditions until a natural disaster occurs or after the government intervenes and the unsafe structures are demolished. Living under such circumstances with children is especially difficult when there is no electricity or running water or hope for a way out of such poverty.

When Jasmin migrated to reside in the United States, she was pleased to see that subsidized housing assistance is provided by the government for low-income households. She visited an acquaintance who lived in a subsidized apartment located in an inner city community. Jasmin learned from her friend that crime frequently occurred in the area. In fact, throughout the years public housing has deteriorated and regarded as a slum environment associated with poor maintenance and high crime. These buildings or communities may be found throughout major cities but, for the most part, many of the housing projects built in the 1950s and 1960s have been torn down. For instance, the Pruitt-Igoe housing project built during that period was demolished. The housing project included 33 buildings with 11-storeys, each situated on 57 acres in the poverty stricken DeSoto-Carr neighborhood outside of St. Louis, MO (Marshall, 2015). The intentions were to replace the deteriorating, crowded houses with better accommodations. However, from 1957, these new buildings began to deteriorate, and the crowded buildings became inundated with vandalism and crime that were encouraged, some believe, by the buildings' design. After spending millions of dollars to address the problem, all buildings were finally demolished by 1973.

Nowadays, instead of building public housing, state and local housing authorities have initiated for persons who qualify to receive Housing Choice Vouchers. This Housing Choice Voucher program is also known as Section 8, a term derived from Section 8 of the

Housing Act. These vouchers are intended to assist low income families, elderly, and the disabled to afford to rent residence that meets the government standards of decency, safety, and sanitary through the private market. Therefore, people in need now have an opportunity to reside in housing wherever they want to as long as the owner of the residence agrees to participate in the housing choice voucher program. A housing subsidy is paid to the landlord on behalf of the family who in turn has to pay the difference between the actual rent and the subsidized amount of the rent. The demand for housing often exceeds the limited budget, so families are often placed on waiting lists. Eligibility for housing is determined by gross income and family size. For the most part, it is limited to United States citizens. However, specified categories of non-citizens with eligible immigration status may qualify for this program (United States Department of Housing and Urban Development, n.d.)

While low income residents have the opportunity of obtaining affordable housing, many landlords have related horror stories on the conditions their houses have been returned back to them after a Housing Choice Voucher occupant leaves. These landlords have also expressed concerns on the bureaucracy that often occurs with local government housing agencies that makes the process more difficult than expected. As a result, many who had originally thought that participating in the Housing Choice Voucher program would be beneficial for both sides have opted out. Of course, with a decreased willingness to participate, there are less housing and a long waiting list of candidates for low income housing. The following website provides information on affordable housing: **http://portal.hud.gov/hudportal/HUD?src=/topics/housing choice voucher program section 8**

Coping with Mental Illness

In Amed's native country, he was not aware of anyone who received treatment from a psychologist or psychiatrists for a mental illness. In fact, he did not know of any psychologist or psychiatrist in his home town. He associated mental illness with some homeless persons he saw who appeared to be disheveled, incoherent, and demonstrating hallucinating behavior. He always wondered how people could decline to such levels where they became disassociated with living a normal life. Amed also noticed that no one appeared interested in helping these mentally ill people who seemed accustomed to walking the streets aimlessly.

Amed and his wife, Rachel, were excitedly anticipating the birth of their first child. They were even more pleased since the birth would take place in the United States. They had obtained asylum and, in addition to fulfilling their desire to migrate, their child would be born in a country with so many opportunities. However, after the baby was born, Amed noticed that his wife did not have any desire to bond with their son. Rachel could not explain why she did not have a need to cuddle her baby who had spent nine months growing inside her. She was also not eager to welcome friends who wanted to visit the family. Rachel found she was more comfortable remaining inside her room instead of interacting with others. On the urging of Amed, Rachel finally decided to see her doctor who referred her to a psychiatrist. She learned that she was suffering from post-partum depression. Postpartum depression occurs when mothers experience psychological disorders after childbirth. Through guidance and continuous treatment, Rachel steadily developed the ability to bond with her baby.

Amed realized that unlike his native country, psychiatrists and psychologists were common throughout the United States. Further, he had often heard others at work talking about having an appointment to see their psychiatrist as if this practice was as normal as visiting a general doctor. People did not seem embarrassed to divulge such information which in Amed's culture would be considered a private family matter. He learned that people seek the services of a psychiatrist for common problems such as someone unable to cope with a death in the family, stress and anxiety, phobias, family relation issues, addictions, desires to enhance performance, need for mental clarity, and mental disorders such as bipolar disorders. Mental health disorders even with psychotic treatment have caused those not taking their drugs to commit serious crimes. In the Aurora theatre shooting in 2012, James Holmes shot up a movie theatre killing many patrons although he was in the care of a psychiatrist before the attack.

Thao (2009) uncovered common barriers in the United States that prevent immigrants from receiving mental health services. First, mental health publications are not commonly found in an immigrant's native language. Also, there would exist difficulties in translating concepts since languages vary from culture to culture. Next, stigma of mental health is a major factor among immigrants because the illness gives an impression that a mentally challenged person is "crazy". People with mental health issues are generally ostracized by communities in some countries (Thao, 2009). Furthermore, in small communities, news on someone's mental health issues may spread quickly, and such rumors could affect a family's reputation when people believe that the illness is hereditary. Of course, such perception would prevent a family member from getting married.

Amed became aware that even the most admired people in the United States seek treatment from psychiatrists. Similar to his wife's condition, he was told that celebrity actress, Brook Shields, experienced postpartum depression, and she publically discussed her medical condition and how she sought treatment to learn and manage her disorder. Amed was also surprised that others were not embarrassed to announce they are seeking treatment for other mental health conditions such as a sex addiction. Whatever the case, psychiatrists are always in demand throughout the United States. For more information on mental health care, see **http://www.mentalhealth.gov/**

Wage Theft

Javier waits, along with others, at a popular spot on the main street every day in hope of getting a day job. If he is lucky to be selected, he knows that he must work very hard for long hours. A day's pay does not amount to much money, but Javier knows that he has no choice. He will have to take whatever job is offered to him since he is an undocumented immigrant. Those who hire such workers at this spot are generally aware of the workers' illegal status. Therefore, while these employers are providing jobs, they benefit from taking advantage of vulnerable immigrants who will work for little or nothing.

Even legal immigrants may be ignorant of labor laws governing their employment, so they too may be taken advantage of at the workplace when their employer commits wage theft. Wage theft occurs when employers withhold wages or deny benefits that are rightfully due to an employee. The illegal action has become prevalent throughout the United States. In Javier's case, he worked overtime without receiving time and a half pay for working the additional hours. Others may be expected to work six or even seven days per week without any lunch break. In addition, wage theft involves failure to pay minimum wage, misclassifying employees, illegal deductions in pay, working off the clock, or not paying the employee at all. Wage theft is common among low wage earners who more often than not are illegal immigrants. Yet, for the most part, although some workers are aware of the laws that protect all employees, they see no problem putting up with the lengthy working hours under difficult conditions. Javier's cousin is one of these workers, and he confessed that it is more important not to jeopardize his job, regardless of workplace difficulties, since it took him a long time to secure employment.

Other workers may not know their rights or where to turn. The UCLA Labor Center's review of wage theft cases uncovered that every week, workers in Los Angeles lost $26.2 million because of wage theft violations. In addition, the UCLA study indicates that day laborers are hired to work in some of the most dangerous jobs at worksites, and there is little meaningful enforcement of health and safety laws. Therefore, day laborers continue to endure unsafe working conditions because of their fear to speak up to avoid firing or not receiving pay for their work.

There may be brave whistle blowers who will report a wage theft experience to the enforcement authorities. However, enforcing the rules is difficult since few people at federal and state regulatory bodies are assigned to address this lengthy process. While the process is taking years to be resolved, businesses may shut down or may be reestablished under a new name. The majority of companies ruled against by the labor commission and courts did not pay back any wages (UCLA Labor Center, n.d.). Therefore 83 percent of workers who filed the court-ordered claim never received a dime.

"Back pay" is a common remedy for wage violations. Back pay is decided by a court to make up the difference between what the employee was paid and the amount he or she should have been paid. Methods of recovering back pay include (a) the Wage and Hour Division supervising payment of back wages, (b) the Secretary of Labor bringing a lawsuit, and (c) an employee files a private lawsuit. A court ruled that a Papa John's pizza franchise should pay its workers nearly $800,000 in unpaid wages due to allegations that the business did not pay overtime to its staff. In another case, a claimant expressed that he worked seven days straight and sometimes 11 hours a day. Although the worker clocked 70 hours a week, he was never paid time-and-a-half for overtime. The worker expressed that sometimes he worked 60 and even 90 days in a row with no days off. This worker joined in a class action lawsuit in expectation of receiving over $20,000 in back pay. For more information on workers' rights, contact the National Consumer League at **http://www.natlconsumersleague.org/worker-rights/148-wage-theft/529-wage-theft-youre-a-victim-now-what**

The Welfare System

Government assistance is not the norm for people living in poverty in Alexandre's birth country. These people are on their own with no expectations to receive government aid. Therefore, day-to-day, they do whatever is necessary to survive. While some will seek household or yard or handyman work for meagre wages, others prefer self-employment in whatever area that will allow them to make money. These are resilient people who do not allow poverty to keep them from enduring. Many will illegally build flimsy structured dwellings on vacant land owned by the government or private persons. It is a difficult life, but the poor somehow manages to deal with their adversities without any government financial intervention

Alexandre perceived immediately that low income people were treated differently in the United States than what he was used to in his country. He was surprised to learn about the public resources that were available to them through the U.S. Welfare program. He noticed that when he went to the grocery store in his neighborhood at the beginning of the month, it was busier than any other time of the month with so many shopping for food. He learned that people were using their monthly welfare cards to shop for food. In addition to the SNAP food program where recipients can use a debit card for their grocery shopping, the 13 U.S. Welfare Programs include; tax credits; housing assistance, supplemental social security for the elderly who are disabled; Pell grants for post-secondary studies; child nutrition programs at schools; WIC programs that provides health food for pregnant women and young children; childcare, etc. In general, conditions for acceptance to the welfare program is limited. However, the conditions of certain welfare programs could include work requirements, job training, school attendance and/or grades obtained, drug and alcohol testing.

Some, like Alexandre, believe that while the welfare system has made lives comfortable, it is ineffective because recipients would rather not get a job or get married in order to avoid losing their benefits. As a result of these issues, the program has led to a dependency rather than motivate the recipients to marry and find jobs.

Furthermore, those dissatisfied with the program argue that the recipients own televisions, air conditioners, and all the other comforts of life. Therefore, some contend that it is not fair to those hard working people who have achieved an equivalent standard of living. In addition, another concern with the Welfare system is a study shows that children of parents on welfare will quite likely participate in the same system when they become parents. As such, a culture where welfare is used in one generation is expected to cause welfare to be used by the next generation (Bacon, 2013). Consequently, it is assumed that children who are raised in a welfare household quite often learn and follow their parents' experiences.

People whose welfare application contains lies about their entitlement to welfare or those whose financial needs have improved but the change is not disclosed are described as committing welfare fraud. For instance, a woman applied for and received welfare for herself and children. The husband returned to the marital home, but the wife failed to divulge her reunion. She was prosecuted and convicted when the department found out the undisclosed change in her status. Another case involved a couple living on a million dollar yacht who were accused of claiming welfare benefits. Often, investigators from the Welfare office make unannounced visits to the recipients' residences. Under the program, the investigators can walk through the house and even look in the closets, trash cans, and other receptacles. Any evidence of violations is sent to the prosecutor for criminal investigation. The website **http://www.welfareinfo.org/welfare-resources/** includes information on the Welfare program.

Chapter 5

Impacted by Race and Gender

Race Based Laws

David had never experienced discrimination until he came to live in the United States. In his country, all races intermingled to form friendships, marriages, and business partnerships. Therefore, it was disconcerting to him when he realized that the laws are not administered equally to all persons in the United States. He became aware that while there are laws, and all is expected to adhere to these laws, instances have shown that minorities such as Blacks, Latinos, Native Americans and others experience the wrath of the justice system while Whites receive a much favorable outcome of their situations. From as far back as the Civil Rights movement, David was informed that Blacks were more than likely to be convicted by all White juries even if it was evident that they were unjustly accused of a crime. On the other hand, during such period, Whites were guaranteed a not guilty verdict although evidence pointed to their guilt. Therefore, David noticed the flaws in the criminal justice system where minorities are disproportionately affected.

According to the San Jose Mercury News (1991) of the 700,000 criminal cases reviewed from California between 1981 and 1990, records showed statistically significant disparities throughout various stages of the criminal justice process. For instance, six percent of Whites, as compared to only four percent of minorities, won "interest of justice" dismissals, in which prosecutors dropped a criminal case entirely. In addition, the study found 20 percent of White defendants charged with crimes providing for the option of diversion received that benefit, while only 14 percent of similarly situated Blacks and 11 percent of similarly situated Latinos were placed in such programs. The same study revealed consistent discrepancies in the treatment of White and non-White criminal defendants at the pretrial negotiation stage of the criminal process. During 1989-1990, a White felony defendant with no criminal record stood a 33 percent chance of having the charge reduced to a misdemeanor or infraction, compared to a 25 percent chance for Blacks or Latinos who committed similar crimes.

A vast body of research identified racial disparities at different phases of the justice system (Kahn and Kirk, 2015) as follows:

- Blacks are more likely to be pulled over and their cars searched without receiving a reason for being stopped. In fact, police are three times more likely to search the cars of Black drivers than stopped Whites.

- Blacks are more likely to be arrested for drug use. They are arrested for drug crimes at twice the rate than Whites who use and sell drugs at comparable rates.

- Black are more likely to be jailed while awaiting trial as noted in a 2014 study in New York. Research suggests that the disparity may be because Black defendants cannot afford to pay bail as their White and non-Black counterparts.

- Blacks are more than likely to be offered a plea deal that includes prison time as opposed to Whites who are more often presented with plea deals with no prison time.

- Blacks may be excluded from juries because of their race. For example, researchers found that North Carolina prosecutors were excluding Blacks from juries in capital cases at twice the rate than other jurors so as to influence deliberations and verdicts. The reasoning is that with a Black juror, Black defendants are less likely to receive the death penalty in capital cases.

- Blacks are more likely to serve longer sentences than Whites for the same offense since prosecutors are expected to file charges against Blacks that carry mandatory minimum sentences.

- Blacks are more than likely to be disenfranchised because of a felony conviction. For instance, the right to vote is revoked in some states.

- Blacks are more than likely to have their probation revoked.

More information on racial disparity may be found on
http://www.businessinsider.com/theres-blatant-inequality-at-nearly-every-phase-of-the-criminal-justice-system-2015-8

Sundown Mentality Persists

When Aswad moved to the United States in 1979, he lived in a community populated by many people from his country along with Americans of different races. Throughout the state, however, he heard that communities were separated based on the color of one's skin. He was informed segregated neighborhoods have been ongoing for many years from the Jim Crow era when Blacks living throughout the south resided 'on the other side of the railway track' away from the White community. He came from a country where there were ethnic tension and a separation of the people. However, he thought he had put community divisions behind him when he came to the United States.

The movie, *A Raisin in the Sun,* depicts the extent that Whites took to keep Blacks from moving into their neighborhoods during the 1950s. This housing segregation has continued throughout the years. As Blacks could afford to purchase homes in neighborhoods where Whites resided, they usually noticed 'for sale' signs going up around the communities as Whites began to sell their homes and move away to other preferred areas. Integration has different meaning for Whites as it does for Blacks (Wilson, 1996). When the number of Black families increased to 3 out of 15 household, 50% of the White respondents said they would not move into the neighborhood and 24% said they would move out.

According to Meyer (2000), African Americans have made great strides toward equal citizenship. However, Whites and African Americans continue to demonstrate an inability to live in the same neighborhoods and this affects race relations in the United States. Meyer concludes that Whites have a negative perception of African Americans and those stereotypical thinking is responsible for the lack of integration found in America's neighborhoods. For example, in 1996, a Black woman from Philadelphia used her Rent Choice voucher to move to a row house in a White neighborhood that contained a large number of properties subsidized by the government for all who qualified. She was welcomed with racial taunts, and two days after she moved in, a neighbor raised the Confederate flag, a symbol of racism and hate. After living under such stressful conditions for seven weeks, she moved out.

In addition, a man in Lena, Louisiana, who was the first African American to move into a home in a White neighborhood was welcomed as a shot gun target when Whites fired on a field adjacent to the man's property before his house was fired upon. The next evening, the residents dressed in Ku Klux Klan robes, went to the adjacent field by the African American's house and shouted "White Power" and "White Knights". Frightened by the events, the family eventually sold their home.

Loewen, (n.d.) uncovered sundown towns from Maine to California. A sundown town is a town, city, or neighborhood in the United States that intentionally maintains an all-White population by excluding people of other races. The term "sundown town" originated from signs that were posted in towns stating that people of color had to leave the town by sundown. Sometimes the towns are known as sunset towns or gray towns because they remain predominantly White by keeping out Blacks and other races by force, or law, or custom. The towns have also managed to put the fear in minorities who are noticed driving through its surroundings after the sun sets. So, minorities who are familiar with these towns know that living in these places would not be an option for them.

During 1934 – 1968, the Federal Housing Administration (FHA) promoted housing segregation when they used race and ethnicity to determine mortgage eligibility. Through the practice of "redlining", the agency was responsible for denying or limiting financial services to certain neighborhoods based on racial or ethnic composition without regard for the qualifications or creditworthiness of the residents. According to Loewen, (n.d.) the FHA publications implied that different races should not share neighborhoods and repeatedly listed neighborhood characteristics such as "inharmonious racial or nationality groups". This practice was outlawed by FHA in 1968. But, Black residents complain that these tactics are still practiced in subtler forms such as through predatory lending agency.

Renters, however, should be aware that the Fair Housing Act protects tenants from discrimination. Under the act, it is illegal for landlords to discriminate on the basis of race or color, national origin, religion, sex, familial status (families with children), or disability. If tenants believe they have been discriminated against when looking for housing, they may contact the local Fair Housing office in their area.

Nowadays, progressive Whites have been encouraged by housing developers to move into predominantly Black occupied areas that have been redeveloped to attract a more affluent population. The reception is quite different since Whites generally do not face the horrific reception that is shown to Blacks who move into predominantly White neighborhoods. With the gentrification of a neighborhood, corporate America becomes willing to build infrastructures that have long been denied when the population was primarily minorities. For more information on the subject see **https://fortworthcivilrights.wordpress.com/the-themes/integration/**

Hands Up Against Racial Profiling!

Peter is an immigrant who has always been proud of his Black heritage. He grew up in a country where people of African descent have been the majority population since slavery. However, throughout the centuries, there has been an influx of immigrants from India, China, Lebanon, Syria and other countries. The intermarrying of these different cultures has produced a nation where the color of one's skin does not affect how people are treated. Since Peter grew up in a middle class, well-known and respected family, he never had any reason to worry about the color of his skin.

Peter received acceptance to a university that is known for its enrollment of the country's top students. He chose instead to continue his education in the United States. After graduating from university with a Bachelor's degree, he entered the university's medical school. In spite of Peter's academic successes, living in the United States for him was challenging especially since it was here he was introduced to prejudice. Peter was bothered that none of his academic accolades mattered in the United States since outside the comfort of the university or hospital where he did his medical residency, he would be subjected to the same racial profiling as other Black and minority groups. So, he had to adjust to the fact that, as a Black male, it would not be unusual for him to be stopped by police officers. In fact, popular entertainer, Chris Rock reported, in April, 2015, that in less than two months, he had been stopped three times by the police. Even Professor Henry Louis Gates, Jr., a long-standing, well-respected Harvard professor, was stopped while going home by a White police officer who felt he did not reside in the Harvard neighborhood. Peter was stopped a number of times when White police officers thought he looked suspicious. Peter was not used to always looking over his shoulder and wondering when the next police stop would occur. However, he tried to be respectful when stopped by the police since he was aware of the many cases where Black men were fatally shot by White police officers.

Some of the more publicized cases of Blacks fatally shot by police officers include Amadou Diallo, an unarmed West African immigrant, who was killed by four New York City police officers' 41 shots. Next, Sean Bell was celebrating a day prior to his wedding when five police officers fired a hail of 50 bullets at him. A more recent case occurred in Ferguson, Missouri, when Michael Brown was shot by a White police officer while the unharmed man raised his two hands in the air. This case influenced more to support the Black Lives Matter Movement that started after the murder of Trayvon Martin. Another case involved Walter Scott who was shot multiple times in the back by a White police officer. Eric Garner presents a different example since he was not shot to death, but he was held in a choke hold by a White police officer although he continuously shouted that he could not breathe. These are just a small fraction of the many incidents which have caused Blacks, especially males, to be on their guard since it is not if but when they will be stopped by the police.

It is every Black mother's nightmare in the United States when their son is out late at night since they hope that there will be no occasion for their child to be stopped by any police officer. To address this matter, Black mothers have seen a need to give their sons "the talk" to inform them what to do in case they are stopped by a police officer while walking on the street or driving in a car. According to the Washington Post, the Justice Department statistics, based on the Police Public Contact Survey, confirms that a Black driver is about 31 percent more likely to be pulled over than a White driver or about 23% more likely than a Latino driver. So "driving while Black" is just not people's opinion, but it is a measurable phenomenon.

Today, "driving while Black" is a common term to signify that Black male drivers tend to be scrutinized by police officers more so than Whites throughout the United States. When a Black driver is pulled over, more often than not, they will be thoroughly scrutinized by police in hope of finding any discrepancies that will warrant an arrest. According to the American Civil Liberties Union (ACLU, 2013), their organization makes all effort to promote good police practices so as to prevent any occurrences of police abuses against citizens. But, too often, patterns of racial profiling, the selective enforcement of laws against people of color, and disturbing stop-

and-frisk policies have demonstrated an unequal effect on certain communities.

Different aspects of racial profiling occur throughout the United States. For instance, in 2006, the police in Tenaha, Texas, stopped, searched, and often seized property from Blacks and Latinos traveling through town although the people were under no suspicion of criminal activity. The police went further to threaten that if these minorities did not turn over their valuables they would be charged with money laundering. Minorities with children were also threatened that their children would be taken away if they did not comply (ALCU, 2013). A well-known racial profiling practice occurred in 2010, when a discriminatory "show me your papers" law was enacted in Arizona that promoted blatant racial profiling against Latinos, Asian Americans, and others presumed to be "foreign" just because of the way they look or sound. (ALCU, 2013).

Peter is now a medical doctor practicing in the United States. Even though he is highly respected at the hospital, he does not expect such reaction to be the same outside of the hospital environment when he wears his civilian clothes. Similar to other Black male professionals, he is regarded as another Black man who will quite likely be stopped by a police officer. It does not matter if the Black man has accomplished success, once he removes his suit and tie or doctor's scrub, and even a police officer's uniform, he may be identified by a police officer as a Black man who is up to no good. Peter realizes that he will continue to fit the profile of someone who is bound to be stopped by the police at some point in time. However, over the years, he has learned to continue to handle himself in the best possible manner by responding courteously to all police officers' questions. So far, his non-confrontational behavior has worked, but he is aware that there could be a time when he may encounter a police officer who is not respectful of his rights. Nevertheless, Peter hopes that he will continue to avoid any confrontation with the police. For tips to address a police stop, see **https://www.brookhavencollege.edu/studentsvcs/police/Pages/stoppedtips.aspx**

Gender Inequality

Aaquila lived in a country where women have no rights. She could not leave the house unless accompanied by her husband or even her young son. She was covered from head to toe with only her eyes visible. As a Muslim woman, Aaquila had no choice but to obey the customs that make women submissive and in fear of punishment in a male dominated society. While there has been an increase over the years of girls attending school, this trend is still greatly resisted by men. Therefore, Aaquila never felt comfortable sending her daughter to school. Her desire to depart from her present environment to make a better life for herself and her family drove her to escape from her native land and eventually settle with her family in the United States.

Living in America meant that Aaquila would have the freedoms that she had often heard about. She could walk on the street by herself whenever she wanted to. She welcomed opportunities for her children, especially for her daughter who now could attend school without fear for her safety. Aaquila continued to dress conservatively but now had the option of wearing a hijab headscarf that could allow her to show her face. Aaquila's strong beliefs superseded any desire to dress as those women in western fashion on the streets. Nevertheless, in spite of the freedoms, life in the United States for her was initially overwhelming because it was a great contrast coming from such an oppressive country. She could not easily disconnect from the customs that had been embedded in her life from childhood. But, she was thankful for the opportunities she now had as a woman.

After living a while in the United States, Aaquila noticed that although women possessed so many freedoms, certain limitations still existed. For example, she often heard on the news that a woman who did the same job as a man would not be paid the same as her male counter path. Hill (2014) reports that there is a pay gap between men and women. However, her research uncovered that a gap also exists based on a woman's race. As a result, African American and Latina women have been paid lower wages than

White and Asian-American women even if they possessed the same educational background.

Aaquila also learned that while there are more women CEOs than before, the ratio of men as CEO or in executive positions have far outweighed the women in leadership roles. A Fortune 500 report indicates that few women are rising to the top of their profession (Fairchild, 2015). Although there were no female CEOs in the Fortune 500 companies 20 years ago, the approximately 25 female CEOs today represent a minor increase. This may be due to the stereotypes that still exist as 34% of respondents to a survey believe that male executives are better than women at assuming risk (Fairchild, 2015).

It was also a surprise to Aaquila that laws needed to be in place to prevent discrimination against women in education and sports activities. Title IX was instigated since there had been a disproportionately lower number of college women participating in college sports prior to 1972. The National Collegiate Athletic Association (NCCA) did not offer scholarships to women or hold championship games for female teams (Wong, 2015). A general survey on the number of women playing sports today has reached an all-time high of 3.27 million. However, an in depth review indicates that gender inequality in sports continues to be severe in certain southern states. Therefore, while Title IX has created opportunities for many women, it does not totally eliminate the disparities.

Aaquila realized that injustices against women have not only been associated with men, but hidden discriminatory practices are noticed between women of different races. She found that White women were regarded more favorably than women of color. For example, an African American woman athlete who has a proven track record of outstanding performances may not be given the same million dollar marketing endorsements as a White woman whose athletic record in comparison may be less successful but she fits the standard look of the all American girl. As such, the White athlete will receive more lucrative endorsements.

When Aaquila compares living in her county to residing in the United States, she affirms that no matter where one lives, all women deserve to be treated equally. Contact information on local agencies that cater to women's needs may be found in public listings on the internet. However, for information on women's rights click on **https://www.aclu.org/issues/womens-rights**

Chapter 6

Influenced by Politics

LGBT Community Making Strides

Devon always felt different ever since he could remember as a child. He wanted to do girlish things and preferred being in the company of girls rather than boys. His parents sensed the difference because Devon did not display masculine behavior as his two older brothers. But, Devon's parents never spoke about the matter. He was popular with the neighborhood children, so no one bothered or joked about his behavior. However, Devon grew up in a homophobic country where the open lifestyle of homosexuals is not tolerated. In fact, mob violence is a common practice if word gets out of a person's homosexuality, and this could result in he or she being brutally beaten or murdered. In one case, a teenager was chopped to death. No laws are in place to protect the rights of this group. Furthermore, homosexuals and lesbians cannot seek assistance from the police because they are considered in violation of the buggery law.

When Devon arrived in the United States, he realized that he could live without having to hide his sexual preference and even get married to a same sex partner. Over the past two decades, State legislatures and voters have made extensive changes in laws determining whether marriage should be restricted to relationships between a man and a woman or if the same rights should be extended to same-sex couples (National Conference of State Legislature, 2014). Previously, 33 states determined that marriage was a relationship between a man and a woman and prohibited same-sex marriages while 17 states and the District of Columbia allowed same-sex marriage. Across the country, there were contrasting state laws which reflected major differences in the people's views toward marriage and same-sex marriage. However, in 2015 the Supreme Court's majority ruled that same sex couples have the right to marry in any state and receive the spouse's benefit similar to their heterosexual counterpart.

Devon lives in a city that has always been receptive to the large Lesbian, Gay, Bisexual, Transgender (LGBT) community that has been responsible for organizing a yearly parade. It was an eye-opening experience for him to attend the parade to see how participants embraced each other in public without fear. They kissed, laughed, and danced to loud music in a festive atmosphere that included floats proceeding from one block to the next. Many were dressed in drag or otherwise female attire. But, more surprising to him was to see representatives participating in the parade from various entities such as politics, education, and private organizations. It was brought to his attention that some floats were funded by government or corporate sponsors.

Devon knows that the rights of the LGBT community have been steadily improving over the years. For instance, he is aware that barriers to adoption still exist in several states, but many same-sex couples have been able to adopt. This is welcome news for Devon who wants to adopt children in the future. One quarter of children living with same-sex couples in the United States have been adopted, according to a research guide from the Georgia State University College of Law. United States Census Bureau data indicates that since 2000, the number of children living with same-sex parents has doubled. The rise of LGBT biological parents has increased that amount. These progressive birth parents are generally considered domestically stable with quality relationship and financial security. Adoptions have increased since some states have changed laws regarding same sex adoption. For example, in 2010, Florida overturned a ban that prevented gays and lesbians from adopting children. The Florida Supreme Court ruled the ban unconstitutional and determined that it denied the "best interests of the child," according to a CNN report. But, same sex adoption continues to be an uphill battle in other states in spite of the 2015 ruling of the Supreme Court to grant same sex couple the right to wed throughout the United States.

While there are laws against discrimination in the United States, Devon knows that, as a gay man living in an imperfect world, he will still encounter people who do not agree with the lifestyle. Reports show that 21 states, Washington, D.C., and Puerto Rico banned discrimination based on sexual orientation. Employment Opportunity Commission (EEOC) ruled that job discrimination against lesbian, gay, bisexual and transgender individuals are classified as a form of sex discrimination. In the case of the United

States armed forces, the "don't ask don't tell" policy, established in 1994, prohibited any homosexual or bisexual enlistee from disclosing his or her sexual orientation or from speaking about any homosexual relationships, including marriages or other familial attributes, while serving in the United States armed forces. However, in 2011, President Obama formally certified that the American military was ready for the repeal of the "don't ask, don't tell" policy. So, service members no longer are forced to hide their sexual preferences in order to serve their country. More information on parades, legal rights of the LGBT community, adoption, may be found at **https://www.aclu.org/issues/lgbt-rights**

1st and 2nd Amendments

Malcolm was not familiar with the United States Constitution. Growing up in another country, he learned about the historical laws of his native land which coincided with that of England since he resided in a Commonwealth country that was formerly a British colony. However, while living in the United States, a number of well-known incidents occurred throughout the country, and the national media coverage of these cases caused him to become familiar with two of the amendments to the United States Constitution - the First Amendment and the Second Amendment.

Malcolm learned that the First Amendment signifies freedom of speech, religion, press, and assembly. This right is expected for all who resides throughout the United States. According to the United States Supreme Court, the First Amendment has become the fortress for protecting the "uninhibited, robust, and wide-open" discussion of controversial and often unpopular issues in public places. Malcolm could understand the need to protect the noted rights, but he could not conceive how freedom of speech would extend to hate groups including White supremacy groups such as the Ku Klux Klan (KKK). He could not comprehend how the KKK possess the same rights as any group to publically make their views known by marching in the streets. He was bothered that in spite of the KKK's longstanding history of committing violence against minorities and their criminal convictions, the group has still maintained the right to openly spread their hate messages and recruit members into their organization.

In spite of the protection of speech, Malcolm notices that this right is constantly challenged. One instance occurred in 2007 when a University of Florida student was stung with a Tasar by police for exercising his First Amendment right of refusing to leave a microphone after he exceeded the allotted time of asking a question to Senator John Kerry. Even Freedom of the Press has been compromised in instances such as when former Attorney General Alberto Gonzales threatened that the government had the right to prosecute journalists who published alleged classified information.

Others may believe that freedom of speech was challenged in the well-known whistleblower cases that include Bradley Manning a/k/a Chelsea Manning, Edward Snowden, and others when the government filed charges against them for releasing confidential documents. As for religious freedom, Hobby Lobby, a religious corporation was one of the 39 non-profit companies that sued the Federal Government on the grounds that it infringed upon the company's religious rights by forcing it to provide contraceptive coverage to employees enrolled in the Affordable Care Act's insurance plans. The Supreme Court subsequently ruled in favor of the non-profit corporations' rights to maintain religious freedom. The right to Freedom of Assembly was challenged during the 2014 demonstrations in Ferguson, Missouri, over the death of Michael Brown. During the initial demonstrations, the crowd faced heavily armed police wearing camouflage mask and body armor in addition to using military firearms, armored vehicles, and throwing tear gas into the crowd to disburse them from participating in their right to assemble.

The Second Amendment includes details on the right to bear arms. Malcolm recognizes that this amendment is constantly quoted by many in defense of their ownership of a firearm whenever opponents voice the need for gun control. Further, the advocacy for the right to bear arms are supported not only by the National Rifle Association and National Association for Gun Rights, but their influential lobbyists in Washington D.C. have ensured that the chances of adopting gun control remain a challenging task to accomplish. As a result, in the meantime, guns continue to be easily accessible to all and even those who have been previously diagnosed as mentally unstable.

As gun sales continue to rise through local gun shows at arenas and even on some church premises, Malcolm sees no resolution in sight to solve the mass shootings that continue to plague the nation throughout the years. For example, in 2005, Jeffrey Weise, 16 years old, murdered his grandfather and his girlfriend along with seven persons at his high school. In 2006, Charles Roberts shot 10 young Amish girls in a schoolhouse. During that year, Jennifer San Marco, a former postal worker, shot and killed seven persons. In 2007,

Seung-Hui Cho opened fire on the Virginia Tech campus killing and injuring a total of 56 persons. The same year, Robert Hawkins opened fire inside Westroad Mall killing 13. In 2008, Charles Tornton shot and killed 8 when he went on a rampage. During 2009, Army psychiatrist, Nidal Hasan, opened fire on an Army base and killed and injured a total of 43 persons. Omar Thornton shot and killed a total of 11 persons during 2010. For 2011, Jared Lougher opened fire and killed and injured a total 19. The trend continued in 2012 as James Holmes opened fire in a movie theatre killing or injuring a total of 70. During the same year, at Newtown school, Adam Lanza shot his mother and went to the Sandy Hook Elementary school where he shot and killed 20 children and six school personnel. Next, but certainly not the last incident, in 2015 Dylann Roof opened fire and killed nine members of a South Carolina church who welcomed him to join their bible study prayer group to worship with them. For information on the Amendments to the Constitution visit the website **http://constitutioncenter.org/constitution/the-amendments**

Religious Inconsistencies

Imran is native of a country where he was afraid to make known his Christian faith. He grew up as a worshiper of the nation's dominant religion. However, he converted to Christianity as an adult when he became familiar with the religion while working as an interpreter. He dared not let this conversion known outside of his house since he would have been considered a traitor. He got married to a Christian woman, Fatima, who, like himself, worshipped in secrecy. Both were familiar with cases where Christians were killed simply because of their religion. So, they continued to engage in the religion of birth to avoid any suspicions and questions. When Imran and Fatima realized that they could no longer live their life with fear of worshiping openly in a church, they decided to visit the United States embassy to apply for asylum. As a result of turmoil and the drastic increases in the murder rate, Imran and Fatima were two of the lucky few to obtain visas to migrate to the United States.

It was a relief for Imran and Fatima when they landed in the United States. This was a country where they felt safer, and they could attend any church they wanted to without living in fear that doing so would cause their deaths. Imran knew that the First Amendment guaranteed freedom of religion. He had the right to worship wherever he wanted to and whenever he wanted to. He was also glad to now reside and work among people with so many diverse religious beliefs. Imran did not lose time in locating a church where he and Fatima could worship. The members of the church were so welcoming, and they went out of their way to provide whatever aid they could to Imran and Fatima. In fact, it was through the assistance of the church that the couple obtained their first jobs in the United States.

One factor that stood out in the couple's church was that he did not see a diverse congregation although the city was comprised of a varied population. Imran noticed the same at another church in the community and mentioned his concern to Fatima. Different races did not seem to attend those Christian churches where he had expected to associate with a diverse congregation. It seemed to simply be the culture that had been embedded in the lives of the population throughout so many years of racial tension. Smietana (2015) reports that Sunday mornings are one of the most segregated hours in America since more than 8 out of 10 churches are filled with one predominant racial group. This condition is acceptable to most of the congregation.

Imran acknowledged that even in his country, religious leaders were expected to possess some comforts in life. However, it was appalling to him the excessive wealth amassed by some of the religious leaders in the United States. He believes that these leaders live a jetsetter lifestyle with mansions and even private aircrafts owned by some. It has been troubling to Imran that such lifestyle contrasts immensely with the teachings of the humble life lived by Christ. Yet, the large congregations attending the churches of these wealthy religious leaders do not seem to mind since they have continued to financially support such opulence without question. Some have thrown more than they can afford in the collection plates while their own financial needs are neglected. CNN reported on the lavish homes of American Catholic Archbishops since 10 lived in homes valued over one million dollars as noted in church and government records. Siebold (2015) wrote about one televangelist who requested for his congregation to donate at least $300 for him to purchase a $65 million private jet. Imran finds it alarming that such behavior continues without any legal ramifications. But, he believes that, in the long run, these religious leaders may not have to answer to the people but a day will certainly come when they will have to answer to their God on their manipulative deeds in achieving such riches.

Another concern of Imran was that in a country that stood for religious freedom, intolerance was evident when it came to persons wearing religious symbols. For instance, a woman was denied employment because she wore a hijab. The United States Supreme Court ruled in her favor. However, her case is just one of many where persons are discriminated against for wearing religious clothing. According to Siedge (2015), Muslim Americans are widely seen as victims of discrimination. Imran also did not expect that Sikhs face racial profiling from law enforcement. In a 2012 survey, 85 percent of Sikhs indicated that they have been stopped and

questioned by law enforcement officers about their immigration status; 73 percent about their nationality; 66 percent about their religious affiliation (Green, 2015). The Equal Employment Opportunity Commission addresses workers' concerns regarding discrimination including when it relates to an employees' religion. The commissions' website is
http://www.eeoc.gov/laws/types/religion.cfm

Power and Corruption

Tessa is used to political corruption in her native country. Since there are no checks and balances to prevent politicians from accumulating wealth from their backdoor connections and secret deals, they are not held accountable for any dishonest practices. Tessa is disturbed that even when a politician's corrupt practices are quite evident and become known to the public, no inquiries or arrests are made. In addition, at the expense of taxpayers, the government officials engage in excessive foreign travels for not only government business but private affairs; receive luxury cars; re-furbish homes in exclusive neighborhoods; and participate in other improprieties. It was frustrating for Tessa that while the government members live wealthy lifestyles, the country continues to face high rates of poverty, unemployment, crime, and indebtedness to international lending organizations. However, Tessa is aware that corruption is not limited to her homeland. For example, under the leadership of Hamid Karzai, Afghanistan was regarded as one of the most corrupt countries. Karzai, himself, was busted for taking bagful of money from the American military, and this was the least of his dishonesty (Becker, 2014). Obviously, Karzai demitted office as a very rich man. Jean Claude Duvalier, former president of Haiti (1971 – 1986) is another leader who enriched himself by embezzling between $300 and $800 million. President Jacob Zumba's multi-million dollar renovation of his luxury estate demonstrates how this leader used money from the taxpayers of South Africa for his personal business.

Tessa did not expect corruption to be prevalent in the United States. However, she realizes that corruption is not restricted to politicians living in developing countries as her own since a number of corrupt cases occurred while she has lived in the United States. She found the difference, though, was that in the developing countries, politicians will shamelessly continue to perform their official duties without any repercussions. However, in the United Sates, politicians have been arrested and usually demit political office. Tessa sees the Jessie Jackson, Jr. case as an example. She had not expected the Illinois congressman would have been charged and found guilty of misusing campaign funds and other financial improprieties. She was also familiar with the Rod Blagojevich case where the former Chicago Governor received a 14 year prison sentence for soliciting bribes for political appointments in addition to other corruption charges. During her discussion with a friend on the topic of corruption, he made her aware of the Kwame Kilpatrick case where, the former mayor of Detroit, Michigan, was sentenced to 28 years in prison when he was found guilty of corruption that included running a criminal enterprise to rob the city of millions of dollars at a time the city was experiencing severe financial hardships. Former Virginia's governor, Robert McDonnell, was sentenced to 24 months in jail after he was convicted of corruption and conspiracy to commit fraud by providing political favors in exchange for over $165,000 in gifts and loans. Tessa is satisfied that the consolation to tax payers is that politicians cannot escape spending time in jail when they are caught and found guilty, and she hopes that such repercussions will eventually occur in her country to eradicate corruption.

Yet, Tessa has noticed how forgiving the American public has been with corrupted politicians because, in spite of imprisonment or public shame, some politicians in the United States have been given the opportunity to re-invent their image and, as a result, have moved on to live successful lives. For instance, John Edwards, a Democratic nominee for Vice President, was indicted on six felony charges for violating multiple federal campaign contribution laws to cover up his extramarital affair. He was found not guilty on one charge, and the judge declared a mistrial on the other five charges. After going through a public disgrace with a trial and extramarital scandal, Edwards returned to working as a successful attorney. Joe Ganim was imprisoned for embezzling taxpayer dollars as mayor of Bridgeport, Connecticut. After spending seven years behind bars for 16 charges of corruption, he re-entered a race for mayor and was voted back into office as Mayor of Bridgeport. Tom DeLay, former Texas congressman, was convicted of money laundering. While out on bail, he showed an act of defiance by writing a book and participated in the popular television program, *Dancing with the Stars*. For information on anti-corruption in government, see **http://anticorruptionact.org/full-text/**

Chapter 7

Parental Challenges

Physical Discipline Is Prohibited

Ella never forgot the physical punishments she received as a child for misbehaving, and this left her with great fear of getting into trouble during that time. But, discipline in her household seemed to be a breeze in comparison to some of her friends in the neighborhood who were severely punished with whatever object their parents first laid their hands on. But, Ella has come to the conclusion that the punishments made her firm yet caring. So, as a parent, she has not hesitated to discipline her two children. She used methods that were not as severe as the punishments she received as a child. After moving to the United States, she realized that disciplinary methods that she was accustomed to in her country may not be suitable.

In many countries, parents, teachers, and even a neighbor can discipline children who misbehave. In contrast, new immigrants, such as Ella, are rudely awakened by knowledge that a parent dare not lay a hand on his or her own child regardless of any behavioral problems. Doing so may be cause for a parent to be arrested and charged with a criminal act. This type of protection is difficult for immigrants to understand. Even slapping is considered a major form of physical child abuse. For instance, a slap to the face of a 6-year-old boy throwing a temper tantrum landed a Boca Raton, Florida woman in jail, according to a Boca Raton Police Department arrest report. The mother faced a child abuse charge when investigators said she slapped the boy after he wanted to watch a LEGO movie instead of doing homework. A Department of Children and Families intake report said the boy had a black-and-blue bruise on the left side of his face from his ear to jaw bone caused by a hit from his mother.

Certain investigations reveal that hitting a child to discipline him or her may change an immediate behavior since the discipline may instill fear that will prevent the child from repeating the behavior. Reports show that striking a child increases negative behaviors such as aggression. As a result, hitting anyone causes a natural hostile reaction along with fear, anger, and resentment. Research further indicates that these emotional reactions affect a child's future behavior and attitudes.

In addition, critics conclude that if the emotional and mental state of the parent is negative and harsh, this may increase the punishment delivered to the child. Organizations such as the Family Research Council have noted that "physical abuse by an angry uncontrolled parent will leave lasting emotional wounds and cultivate bitterness and resentment within a child," and further, "reactive impulsive hitting after losing control due to anger is unquestionably the wrong way for a parent to use corporal punishment." (Russell, 2009). As a result of the negative outcomes identified by research as it relates to disciplining children, many parents in the United States believe that it is wrong to discipline their children (Examiner, 2010).

Ella had to get used to the typical reactions in the United States that children should be punished without the use of physical measures. According to Russell (2009), research overwhelmingly shows that there are alternatives to spanking that are more effective in raising and disciplining a child. Methods may include but not limited to: (a) calling time out by having the child stay by himself or herself in a solitary location for a short period of time; (b) making the child perform a house duty such as cleaning his or her room; (c) taking away privileges such as cell phone or viewing television; (d) forbidding weekend activities with friends. For more information on children services visit **http://www.acf.hhs.gov/**

Teenagers Adjustment Issues

Jessica wanted to fit in so badly with the students at her high school. She recently arrived in the United States and tried to get rid of her accent so she could sound similar to her peers. She wanted to begin dressing like them so that she did not appear as the odd ball out. She wanted to be a part of the clique who appeared to have so much fun during the weekends. So, Jessica did all that was possible to fit in. She did not think it would be so difficult in fitting in, but it was for her. While attending high school in her native country, she was always an "A" student. However, achieving top grades no longer was her priority. Changing her image by conforming to the lifestyle of her peers was now her main concern. Jessica wished her parents knew that similar to them, she was also experiencing difficulties in adjusting to a new life in the United States.

McCarthy (2003), research confirms that children, especially adolescent, experience great stress that may come from leaving a familiar social context and extended family network. Adapting to a new environment, culture, and language, or from harsh conditions endured before or during the transitional journey could add to the stress. For instance, attending school in the United States is challenging especially for those adolescent whose first language is not English. Immigrant children may be alienated from school and rejected by their native-born peers because of their lack of fluency in English or their different cultural practices (McCarthy, 2003). They not only have to adapt to a new curriculum and standardized exams but to the culture of American students. Some, such as Jessica, do so by changing their style of dressing to appear more Americanized. Boys wear their pants without belts thereby showing their underwear. Some do not know the history of this dress code and, if they are aware, they are not concerned as long as they look like they fit in. Experts agree that being connected and accepted is an important component of adolescent development (McCarthy, 2003).

But, when parents experience any conflicts with their children, the new behavior can be felt by the parent as disrespect in not understanding the parents' justification and sacrifice in coming to the new country. Parents such as Jessica's should realize that, like themselves, their children are also experiencing stress in adapting to a new country. The challenge is for the parents to adapt to their child's needs by finding reasonable methods to support cultural expectations since it is quite likely their children will be affected and changed by the new host culture (Direnfeld, n.d.). Parents should not have a false impression that their child could possibly be affected but rather how and to what degree they will be affected. Those stern immigrant parents whose culture requires complete obedience from their children should consider softening their approach since this firm discipline will not work for children socialized in western culture where individual freedom is valued and rewarded. Direnfeld (n.d.) suggests that instead, immigrant parents should be aware that even the most obedient child's outlook will change, so parents should recognize this new environment and consider solutions to minimize the risk of conflict with their children. If parents come to terms with this expectation, then they can form a close relationship rather than push their child away if they continue to control.

Another difficulty is that parents may become dissatisfied with their children's quicker acculturation and apparent rejection of the family's own ethnic culture. For instance, Jessica's mother, Yohanna, noticed that since her daughter began attending an American school and learned English, she no longer wanted to communicate with her in Spanish. McCarthy (2003) mentions that immigrant children are often forced to make a painful, emotional choice between their parents' culture and the mainstream norms they are exposed to in school. Yohanna was taking an ESL class to improve her English and learning the new language was very difficult for her. She often went to Jessica for help, but her daughter never seemed to be able to find the time to help her mother. Many immigrant parents, such as Yohanna, experience such disconnect from their children who seem to no longer have time for them. Tips for immigrant parents may be found at: **http://www.thelearningcommunity.us/resources-by-format/tips-for-parents/diverse-families/immigrant-families.aspx**

Get Involved in Child's Education

In some cultures, parents believe that their only responsibility is to ensure that their child goes to school. They think that only the teacher is responsible for educating children. This was what Li always thought until she migrated to the United States with her children. She learned that not only teachers, but parents should take part in their child's education. Some immigrants, similar to Li, may come from a culture where they expect to rely on the teacher to educate children. As a result, taking an active role in their child's education is a new concept that they are not used to doing.

Li was made aware that it is important for parents to read to their children at an early age so that children develop an appreciation for reading. This bonding would have been difficult for Li to do because even before migrating to the United States, she had difficulties reading in her native language. Therefore, reading to her child even in her native language would have presented a challenge. Her inability to read well posed another disadvantage for Li who would have liked to help her children with their homework but could not do so due to her limited education and English language ability. Limited English also prevented Li from initially going to Parent Teachers' Association (PTA) meetings or communicating with her children's teachers or becoming a chaperone on school trips. Li was taking English classes but became discouraged since her children's level of English seemed to be more advanced than her knowledge. Nevertheless, Li hoped that she could at least learn as much English so that she could become comfortable getting involved in her children's education, and also develop the confidence to take her children to the library, tour educational sites, and perform other duties that would be beneficial to her children's education.

Parents in a study expressed disappointment that they are unable to help their children with schoolwork (Lake, Snell, et. al. 2006). One helpless situation is when a parent does not speak English. For second language learners, children tend to acquire English faster than their parents and this proficiency places their parents at a disadvantage in helping with homework. Some will persist in their efforts to learn English, so they can help their children. However, this attempt eventually becomes frustrating for the parent causing them to stop trying to help their children. Lake, Snell, et. al.(2006) also report that a parent's lack of education in their native country adds to their inability to help their children. So, they do not have the knowledge to tutor their children when needed. Also, while there may be misconceptions among some teachers and educators that certain parents may not care since they make no attempt to communicate with school personnel, the reality is that immigrant parents may feel intimidated interacting with their child's teacher or speaking to school officials. This embarrassment extends to their absences in volunteering in their child's classroom or attending PTA meetings to avoid a social atmosphere where they may be expected to communicate.

In addition, Li became aware that she should look out for her children's report cards because she would have to review and sign them to acknowledge receipt. Ironically, her children assisted her in understanding the contents of the report card because she was not familiar with the significance of the letter grades. She knows that she will have to rely on her children to understand the educational system and their progress. For instance, when Li finally began attending the PTA meetings, her children assisted in interpreting the conversation with their teachers. Alvarez (1995) mentions that such responsibility forces the adults to be dependent and the children to take charge. In addition, mental health specialists indicate this type of parental reliance can damage the fragile structure transitioning families by leaving parents feeling incompetent and children feeling anxious. However, Alvarez (1995) reports some children who interpret for their parents enjoy having such power. Li hopes that learning English will indicate to her children the effort she is making so that she will eventually not have to depend on them to interpret for her. Many school districts provide programs to assist immigrant parents to become familiar with the school system, so it is important to contact a child's school for information on parental workshops.

References

Abelson, R. (2009). *Harvard medical study links lack of insurance to 45,000 United States deaths a year.* New York Times

ACLU, (2013). *Race and criminal justice,* Retrieved January 19, 2014 from http://www.aclu.org/criminal-law-reform/race-and-criminal-justice

Alston, F. (2010). *Latchkey children.* Retrieved September 27, 2015 from http://www.education.com/reference/article/Ref_Latch_Key_Children/

American Federation of Teachers. (2009).*Importing educators causes and consequences of international teacher recruitment.* Retrieved April 10, 2014 from https://www.aft.org/pdfs/international/importingeducators0609.pdf

American Society for the Protection of Cruelty to Animals, (n.d.). *Birds on factory farms.* Retrieved on January 15, 2015 from https://www.aspca.org

Amusing Planet (2013). *Kids risking their lives to reach school.* Retrieved January (2014) from http://www.amusingplanet.com/2013/03/kids-risking-their-lives-to-reach-school.html

Anti Defamation League (2013). *Religion in the public schools. Prayer in public schools.* Retrieved September 6, 2015 from http://archive.adl.org/religion_ps_2004/prayer.html#.Vez0yxFVikq

Bacon, J. (2013). *Welfare dependency breeds more welfare dependency.* Retrieved January 23, 2016 from http://www.baconsrebellion.com/2013/07/welfare-dependency-breeds-more-welfare-dependency.html

Bazar, E. (2008). *Schools in need employ teachers from overseas.* USA Today News

Becker, S. (2014). *The 10 most corrupt countries in the world.* Retrieved March 18, 2015 from http://www.cheatsheet.com/business/7-most-corrupt-countries.html/?a=viewall

Bell, T. (2012). *Immigrants face cold reality of Maine winter.* Maine Sunday Telegram

Bello, M. (2011). *Report: Child homelessness up 33% in 3 years.* USA Today News.

Berg, T. (2014). *Most minor league baseball players earn less than half as much as fast-food workers.* USA Today – Forthewin. Retrieved September 1, 2015 from http://ftw.usatoday.com/2014/03/minor-leaguers-working-poor-lawsuit-mlb-bud-selig

Bidgood, J. (2013). *Helping immigrants warm to winter.* The New York Times.

Brilliant Earth (n.d.). *Labor & community,* Retrieved February, 2014 from http://www.brilliantearth.com/conflict-diamond-child-labor/

Burke, P. (2014). *Boy, 4, mauled to death by dog in southwest Miami-Dade County.* WPLG Local 10 News. Retrieved January 19, 2015 from http://www.local10.com/news/child-mauled-to-death-by-dog-in-southwest-miamidade-county/27455094

Center for Disease Control (2014). *Fact sheets - Underage drinking.* Retrieved March 13, 2014 from http://www.cdc.gov/alcohol/fact-sheets/underage-drinking.htm

Chaiklin, H (n.d.). *Ethnic minorities.* Retrieved March, 2014, from *http://www.scholastic.com/teachers/article/ethnic-minorities*

Cohn, D'Vera (2014). *Race and ethnicity, U.S. Census.* Retrieved August, 2015 from http://www.pewresearch.org/fact-tank/2014/05/05/millions-of-americans-changed-their- racial-or-ethnic-identity-from-one-census-to-the-next/

Dennis, A. and Braiker, B. (2009). *Secret drinking: A mother's struggle.* People's Magazine. Retrieved March 13, 2014 from http://www.people.com/people/article/0,,20317293,00.html

Devine, C. (n.d.). *Time pressures on employed parents affect families' diets*. Retrieved September 28, 2015 from http://www.human.cornell.edu/outreach/upload/CHE_DNS_Devine_Time.pdf

Diakanwa, D. (2011). *Adjusting and integration new immigrants in the American culture*. Presented at NACSW Convention, Pittsburgh, P.A . October, 2011

Direnfeld, G. (n.d.). *Issues for immigrant parents and their children*. Retrieved January 28, 2015 from http://www.yoursocialworker.com/p-   articles/immigrant-family-adaptation.pdf

Dogbites.org (2014). *2013 Statistics*. Retrieved on January 19, 2015 from http://www.dogsbite.org/dog-bite-statistics-fatalities-2013.php

Donald, B. (20 13). *Inequality in schools threatens United States prosperity*. Retrieved February 9, 2014 from http://news.stanford.edu/news/2013/february/education-equity-report-022013.html

Ellis, B. (2013). *Government reports drop in number of homeless*, CNN Money. Retrieved February 15, 2014 from http://money.cnn.com/2013/11/21/pf/homelessness/index.html

Examiner.com (2010). *Discipline is not child abuse*. Retrieved January 26, 2014 from http://www.examiner.com/article/discipline-is-not-child-abuse

Fairchild, C. (2015). *Why so few women are CEO*. Fortune. Retrieved July 17, 2015 from   http://fortune.com/2015/01/14/why-so-few-women-ceos/

Gambone, G. (n.d.). *What is a cash worker?* Retrieved January 7th, 2016 from http://smallbusiness.chron.com/cash-worker-15878.html

Ganim, S. (2014). *CNN analysis: Some college athletes play like adults, read like 5th-graders*. Retrieved March 6, 2014 from http://www.cnn.com/2014/01/07/us/ncaa-athletes-reading-scores/index.html

Ganim, S. (2014). *Former UNC athlete sues school over academic scandal.* Retrieved January 19, 2015 from http://www.cnn.com/2014/11/07/us/unc-academic-scandal/

Gann, C. (2011). *Man dies from toothache couldn't afford meds.* ABC News Medical Unit.

Giraud, J. (2013). *America's homeless children - unseen, but counted.* Huffington Post. Retrieved February 15, 2014 from http://www.huffingtonpost.com/jeanmichel-giraud/americas-homeless-childre_b_4310821.html

Goffe, L (2014) *The Harlem gentrification: From black to white. New African.* Retrieved January 28, 2015 from http://newafricanmagazine.com/harlem-gentrification-black-white/

Gonzales, R. (2010). *Investing in the American DREAM.* Retrieved from http://www.immigrationpolicy.org/perspectives/investing-american-dream

Goode Bryant, L. and Poitras, L. (2003). *Flag wars.* PBS documentary

Green, E. (2015). *The trouble with wearing turbans in America.* The Atlantic. Retrieved September 12, 2015 from http://www.theatlantic.com/politics/archive/2015/01/the-trouble-with-wearing-turbans-in-america/384832/

Green and Rabin (2013). *City of Miami looks into park hiring practices.* Retrieved February 12, 2014 from http://www.miamiherald.com

Greendoors (n.d.).*Veteran homelessness facts.* Retrieved February 16, 2014 from http://www.greendoors.org/facts/veteran-homelessness.php

Hill, C. (2014). *How does race affect the gender wage gap?* Huffington Post. Retrieved July 17, 2015 from http://www.huffingtonpost.com/catherine-hill/how-does-race-affect-the-gender-wage-gap_b_5087132.html

Homeroom, (2013) *High school graduation rate at highest level in three decades.* Retrieved February1, 2014 from http://www.ed.gov/blog/2013/01/high-school-graduation-rate-at-highest-level-in-three-decades/

Hurtado-de-Mendoza A., Gonzales, F., et. al. (2014). *Social isolation and perceived barriers establishing social networks among Latina immigrants.* Retrieved July 5, 2015 http://www.ncbi.nlm.nih.gov/pubmed/24402726

Immigration Council (2012). *Economic benefits of granting deferred action to unauthorized immigrants brought to U.S. as youth.* Retrieved January 4, /2016 from http://www.immigrationpolicy.org/just-facts/economic-benefits-granting-deferred-action-unauthorized-immigrants-brought-us-youth

Ingraham, C. (2014. *You really can get pulled over for driving while black, federal statistics show.* Washington Post. Retrieved February 24, 2015 from http://www.washingtonpost.com/blogs/wonkblog/wp/2014/09/09/you-really-can-get-pulled-over-for-driving-while-black-federal-statistics-show/

Johnson, A. (n.d.). *9 credit-buildings tips for US immigrants.* Retrieved May 11, 2014 from http://www.creditcards.com/credit-card-news/9-credit-building-tips-for-us-immigrants-1

Kahn, A. & Kirk, C. (2015).*There's blatant inequality at nearly every phase of the criminal justice system.* Business Insider. Retrieved August 28, 2015 from http://www.businessinsider.com

Kane, D. and Stancil, J. (2014). *Fake-class scheme aided UNC players' eligibility, Wainstein report says.* The News & Observer. Retrieved January 19, 2015 from http://www.newsobserver.com/

Kantrowitz, M. (2009). *Why do students drop out of college?* Retrieved October 9, 2015 from http://www.fastweb.com/financial-aid/articles/why-do-students-drop-out-of-college

Kirby, S. (2012). *A Look at the racial disparities inherent in our nation's criminal-justice system.* Retrieved March 7, 2014 from http://www.americanprogress.org/issues/race/news/2012/03/13

Lake, Snell, et. al (2006). *Living in America: Challenges facing new immigrants and refugees.* Robert Wood Johnson Foundation.

Landau, E. (2009). *How the 'fame motive' makes you want to be a star.* CNN. Retrieved August 31, 2015 from http://www.cnn.com/2009/HEALTH/10/28/psychology.fame.celebrity/

Leadership Conference (n.d.) *Justice on trial: Racial disparities in the American Criminal Justice System,* Retrieved January 19, 2014 from http://www.civilrights.org/publications/justice-on-trial/

Leitsinger, M. (2011). *Foreign teachers' American dreams vanish in a flash.* Retrieved May 10, 2014 from http://www.nbcnews.com/id/44708445/ns/us_news-education_nation/t/foreign-teachers-american-dreams-vanish-flash/#.VsxhB30rIdU

Letts (2008). *An Immigrant's adjustment to American life.* Retrieved March 2, 2014 from http://voices.yahoo.com/an-immigrants-adjustment-american-life-1014487.html?cat=9

Lewin, T. (2011). *Study finds family connections give big advantage in college admissions.* Retrieved March 12, 2015 from www.nytimes.com

Lin, J. (2010). *Honor or abandon: Societies' treatment of elderly intrigues scholar.* Retrieved January 6, 2016 from http://newsroom.ucla.edu/stories/jared-diamond-on-aging-150571

Loewen, J. (2005). *Sundown towns: A hidden dimension of American racism.* The New Press: New York, N.Y.

Marshall, C. (2015). *Pruitt-Igoe: the troubled high-rise that came to define urban America – a history of cities in 50 buildings, day 21.* The Rockefeller Foundation. Retrieved March 11, 2014 from http://www.theguardian.com/cities/2015/apr/22/pruitt-igoe-high-rise-urban-america-history-cities

Massachusetts Immigrant and Refugee Advocacy Coalition (n.d.). *Back to the office: career resources for immigrants and refugee professionals.* Retrieved March 2, 2014 from http://www.miracoalition.org/en/workforce-dev/back-to-the-office

McCammon, S. (n.d.). *Challenges faced by immigrant teens.* Global Post. Retrieved on September 13, 2015 http://everydaylife.globalpost.com/challenges-faced-immigrant-teens-17281.html

McCarthy, K (2003). *Adaptation of immigrant children to the United States: A review of the literature.* Retrieved January 27, 2015 from http://crcw.princeton.edu/workingpapers/WP98-03-McCarthy.pdf

Meyer, S. (2000). *As long as they don't move next door.* Rowman & Littlefield Publishers, Inc.: Lantham, MD

Murray, L. (2007. *Factory-farmed chickens: Their difficult lives and deaths.* Encyclopedia Britannica Advocacy for Animals. Retrieved January 17, 2015 from http://advocacy.britannica.com

National Conference of State Legislature (2014). *Defining marriage: State defense of marriage laws and same-sex marriage.* Retrieved March 18, 2014 from http://www.ncsl.org/research/human-services/same-sex-marriage-overview.aspx

National Institute of Alcohol Abuse (2013).*College drinking.* Retrieved March 13, 2014 from http://www.niaaa.nih.gov/alcohol-health/special-populations-co-occurring-disorders/college-drinking

Poon, L. (2015). *Why won't you be my neighbor?* Retrieved on September 26, 2015 from   http://www.citylab.com/housing/2015/08/why-wont-you-be-my-neighbor/401762/

Priven, J. (2005). *Hello! USA: Everyday living for international residents and visitors.* Hello America Inc; Bethesda: MD

Rampell, C. (2013). *Path to United States practice is long slog to foreign doctors.* The New York Times

Restuccia, D. (2014). *A study on the changing racial makeup of 'the next America'.* Retrieved August 30, 2014 from http://www.huffingtonpost.com/2014/04/13/changing-racial-makeup-_n_5142462.html

Robinson, J. (2008). *What you need to know about the beef industry.* Mother Earth News. Retrieved January 15, 2015 from http://www.motherearthnews.com/

Russell, R. (2009), *Is slapping a child considered "Child Abuse"?* Prevent Child Abuse. Retrieved January 26, 2014 from http://preventchildabusenj.org/blog/2011/02/09/is-slapping-a-child-considered-child-abuse/

Schargel, F. (2013). *The real reasons children drop out of school* Retrieved on February 2, 2014 from http://www.huffingtonpost.com/franklin-schargel/the-real-reasons-children-drop-out-of-school_b_4093876.html

Sheehy, K (2014). *How immigrants without legal status can pay for college.* Retrieve January 5th, 2016 from http://www.usnews.com/education/best-colleges/paying-for-college/articles/2014/08/15/how-immigrants-without-legal-status-can-pay-forcollege?page=2

Siebold, S. (2015). *The biggest scam of all: Pastor Creflo Dollar will get his $65 million luxury jet.* Huffington Post. Retrieved September 12, 2015 from http://www.huffingtonpost.com/steve-siebold/the-biggest-scam-of-all-p_b_7521170.html

Singh Miller, R. (2011). *Student credit card use could cause problems later.* U. S. News and World Report

Smietana, B. (2015. *Sunday morning segregation: most worshipers feel their church has enough diversity.* Christianity Today. Retrieved September 11, 2015 from http://www.christianitytoday.com/gleanings/2015/january/sunday-morning-segregation-most-worshipers-church-diversity.html

Smithsonian (n.d.). *Thanksgiving in North America: From local harvests to national holiday.* Retrieved April 27, 2014 from http://www.si.edu/Encyclopedia_SI/nmah/thanks.htm

Steinmetz, K. (2014). *Survey: 1 in 3 Americans have more credit card debt than savings.* Retrieved May 11, 2014 from http://finance.yahoo.com/news/survey-1-3-americans-more-213431025.html

Strauss, V. (2013). *Record number of homeless children enrolled in public schools, new data show.* The Washington Post.

Strauss, V. (2012). *Why education inequality persists - and how to fix it.* The Washington Post.

Sullum, J. (2014). *Life in prison for pot and other travesties of marijuana prohibition.* Retrieved July 30, 2015 from http://www.forbes.com/sites/jacobsullum/2014/09/04/life-in-prison-for-pot-and-other-travesties-of-marijuana-prohibition/

Swarts, P. (2015). *Eric Holder's Justice Department rocked by nepotism charges.* Washington Times. Retrieved on February 6th, 2015 from http://www.washingtontimes.com/news/2015/feb/4/justice-dept-official-accused-nepotism-son-hire-ig/?page=all

Thao, M. (2009). *Immigrant and refugee mental health. Best practices in meeting the needs of immigrants and refugees.* Retrieved on October 5, 2015 from http://www.wilder.org/

UCLA Labor Center (n.d.). *What is wage theft?* Retrieved January 21, 2016 from http://www.labor.ucla.edu/wage-theft/

Ulloa, J. (2011). *Convict couldn't handle being free.* Retrieved March 6, 2014 from http://www.mysanantonio.com/news/local_news/article/

United States Department of Housing and Urban Development (n.d.). *Housing choice vouchers fact sheet.* Retrieved on February 26, 2015 from http://portal.hud.gov/hudportal/HUD?src=/topics/housing_choice_voucher_program_section_8

University of Minnesota (n.d.). *Resources about winter weather and carbon monoxide address preparedness needs of new immigrants.* Retrieved March 8, 2014 from http://www.cidrap.umn.edu/practice/resources-about-winter-weather-and-carbon-monoxide-address-preparedness-needs-new

Valliant, M. (2014). *Top 10 reasons why organic food is more expensive.* Retrieved January 18, 2015 from http://www.hellawella.com/

Vasquez, M. (2015). *The questions to ask before enrolling.* Retrieved July 18, 2015 from http://pubsys.miamiherald.com/static/media/projects/2015/higher-ed-hustle/protecting-yourself.html

Vedantam, S. (2016). *Is there a connection between college football games and risks for rape?* NPR. Retrieved February 17, 2015 from http://www.npr.org/2016/02/17/467036661/research-explores-connection-between-college-football-games-and-sexual-assault-r

Wiggins, J (2009). *Top five court cases that changed religion in school.* Retrieved April 26, 2014 from http://www.afa.net/Blogs/BlogPost.aspx?id=2147486481

Wilkerson, M. (2011). *How celebrities affect society.* Retrieved March 6, 2014 from http://www.lifepaths360.com/index.php/how-celebrities-affect-society-4191/

Wilson, C (1996). *Racism: from slavery to advanced capitalism.* SAGE Publication. Thousand Oaks, CA

Wong, A. (2015). *Where girls are missing out on high school sports.* The Atlantic. Retrieved July 17, 2017 from http://www.theatlantic.com/education/archive/2015/06/girls-high-school-sports-inequality/396782/

Yildiz, N. (2010). *Reducing brain waste: skilled immigrants and the recognition of foreign credentials in the United States.* World Education Services http://www.wes.org/community/evaluation/ForeignCredentialRecognitionUS.pdf

www.ingramcontent.com/pod-product-compliance
Lightning Source LLC
Chambersburg PA
CBHW020516290526
45786CB00002B/631